Theoretical Anthropology or How to Observe a Human Being

For Catherine Beaugrand

Research, Innovative Theories and Methods in Social Sciences and Humanities Set

coordinated by
Albert Piette and Emmanuelle Savignac

Volume 1

Theoretical Anthropology or How to Observe a Human Being

Albert Piette

WILEY

First published 2019 in Great Britain and the United States by ISTE Ltd and John Wiley & Sons, Inc.

ISTE Ltd
27-37 St George's Road
London SW19 4EU
UK

www.iste.co.uk

John Wiley & Sons, Inc.
111 River Street
Hoboken, NJ 07030
USA

www.wiley.com

Library of Congress Control Number: 2019931844

British Library Cataloguing-in-Publication Data
A CIP record for this book is available from the British Library
ISBN 978-1-78630-413-1

Contents

Preface

The Quest of Anthropologicality

*I am learning how to see. I'm starting. It's still not going well.
But I want to make the most of my time.*

Rainer Maria RILKE

*I come to one of the memoir writers' difficulties—one of the
reasons why, though I read so many, so many are failures. They
leave out the person to whom things happened. The reason is
that it is so difficult to describe any human being. So they say:
"This is what happened"; but they do not say what the person
was like to whom it happened.*

Virginia WOOLF

*Perhaps we are too well aware that an enormous stock of facts
and theories has been amassed, and that in thumbing through
the encyclopedias we may find hundreds of names and words
that represent this potential wealth; and we are too sure that we
can always find someone somewhere who, if only to impress us,
will be glad to enlighten us on any subject whatsoever. And we
promptly withdraw our attention from most of the things that
begin to arouse it, thinking of the learned men who must have
explored or disposed of the event that just stirred our
intelligence. But such caution is sometimes laziness; and
moreover, there is no proof that everything has really been
examined, and in all its aspect.*

Paul VALÉRY[1]

---

1 Quotes drawn from French books or articles have been translated by the author, in cases
where they have not already been published in English.

Several years ago, in preparation for my doctoral thesis, I observed some carnival parades in Belgium. It was mostly the differences in body language or gestures among the participants that caught my attention. Afterwards, I criticized the ethnographic approach as a series of steps that lost first the details and ultimately the human being. When I later understood the significance of considering an individual, one at a time, I observed a priest for a week in Normandy in order to understand some modalities with which humans are present in a situation or move on to another. Subsequently, I slowly understood that an anthropological specificity of research should only concern human beings as they are human beings and not because they play a specific role, carry out a specific activity, or are situated in a given context, and even less so because they belong to a specific culture or social group. Along the way, in several books in debates with Malinowski, Goffman, ethnomethodology, Bourdieu, Latour, but also the "ontological turn", I kept thinking critically – a reflection which I will not refer to here – about the holistic, relationist and interactionist angle of the social sciences and social anthropology in particular[2].

It became even clearer to me that the human beings presented in these terms are or should be the focus of anthropology when, on January 19, 2016, Catherine Beaugrand and Samuel Dématraz filmed me uninterruptedly for nearly 12 hours, and I later watched and re-watched the complete and unedited video. This seems very important to me: I would not have written this book and elaborated the theory that readers will discover without the heuristic force of this video or if I had not been struck by what the series of those images showed, even if this book is not directly related to this film. The risk of losing the human entity is ever present as we carry out research, from the choice of the subject to the final draft. An uninterrupted film that focuses on one individual and the description of a series of instants represent a radical way of not losing him[3] and grasping him in his entirety and in the abundance of details. Such is my fascination with "anthropo-logy" and its ambition, namely the human being, which it occasionally expresses but does not really carry out until the very end. The intuition that lies in presenting a human being as a "volume" in his entirety, as we will see, with this

---

2 I have elaborated on these thoughts in several works in French [PIE 96, PIE 14a]. They can also be found in *Existence in the Details* and *Separate Humans* [PIE 15, PIE 16].

3 The use of the male pronoun in this work is intended to be personal but not gender-specific, and should be read as "he or she" and "him or her" throughout.

anthropological aim dates back to a few years before this filmic experimentation.

I am writing these sentences after teaching a class called "Anthropology of daily life" in the department of anthropology of the University of Paris Nanterre. I explained to my students that these three words should be synonymous. There is nothing that is not daily life. Besides, I prefer the word "existence" to "life". As I tell my students, our existence is a series of instants, moments and situations. Something seems to be a principle for a work of this kind: an observer observes only an individual at a time, in a situation, then in another, meeting people, then leaving them and meeting other people, and then leaving them too. Thus, existence is the existence of necessarily separate individuals, which anthropologists should prioritize over what happens to them or surrounds them.

However, anthropology, with its history and institutions, does not lie here. Anthropology is not volumological, if I may say, and it does not consider human beings in a radical manner. The game of synonyms does not work. Anthropology is especially concerned with situations that are thematically chosen and shared by individuals who carry out religious, political, or technological activities, etc. Or it looks for topics that overlap several situations. It is first interested in actions, interactions, relations and cultures. A strong trend, still ongoing in anthropology, involves regarding humans as individuals who share social or cultural characteristics. For example, when anthropology focuses on an individual or on one of his specific activities or experiences, it actually "runs through" him to bypass him, leave him and especially to grasp other things, for example interactions, political systems and social life.

Look at a human being himself, and learn to see him. This is what I tell my students time and again. As I taught, my students shared things: a university application to the department of anthropology, a skill concerning what is appropriate in class. However, they are all different. Is this obvious? For each, these shared things naturally do not represent the whole volume, as they are mixed to some other dimensions. Before leaving, I told my students that the following week they would be the same, or nearly the same, and that they would come across other volumes, see, listen and be affected, but only a little. Everyone is in a continuity that makes him remain nearly the same after each moment or situation. It took me a long time to understand this properly. I think that this element, which may seem obvious, has significant consequences on the descriptions and analyses of anthropologists.

This book is presented as a "treatise" that includes a series of paragraphs and subparagraphs preceded by numbers. I chose this structure to allow readers to read slowly and hierarchically, so that they could proceed point by point. This book includes seven parts of different lengths. The first is this presentation to the reader. The second is an introduction. There, I present the common thread of this book, i.e. an "anthropological reversal" operation that involves foregrounding human entities in their entirety, namely modifying the way in which anthropology structures in most cases its research, as it fragments the human being, focusing on his parts, and dilutes him in social relations and contexts. Thus, I attempt to present the human volume as the very focus of anthropology and, in fact, its very scale. This introduction represents in a sense the theory of this book. The third part, that is, the first chapter, constitutes its theory. This is the development of the thesis, which describes the reality of a volume, considered and simultaneously theorized by the anthropologist, who recalls that the Greek verb *théôréô* means to look, to examine and to contemplate. This is the very question tackled by "theoretical anthropology", which attempts, according to the meaning of these two words, to consider a human being and to represent a human science that targets human beings. A volume is presented as an individual unity separate from the others. As a separate unit, he is not necessarily closed, but simply in "attempts" of relations with others. By focusing on a volume in and of himself, let us say the anthropological volume, I try to retrieve his constitutive elements, as their combinations characterize moments of presence. Just as I point out how relevant it is to incorporate into a whole volume as many of his components as possible, specifically both those that define his active part and those that define his passive part, I debate those theories based in most cases on a specific element and the difficulty they pose for any description of the complexity of moments of presence. In a volume, there are two other very significant elements: consistency and continuity. Specifically, based on the "style" and stylistic expressions that accompany actions, words or emotions, I will try to show how these are "retained" in and by a volume. This is a point that contradicts the schools of thought – which often inspire anthropologists – that emphasize the idea of freedom, invention or constantly emerging flow. The other element is lessereity as the ability of a volume to decrease and reduce what happens, and therefore "appropriate" it. I consider lessereity, which I present in its different forms, as a key principle that governs the human volume. In the fourth part, that is, the second chapter, I introduce some drawings, or rather some sketches or outlines, with the aim of illustrating what a human volume is and showing more instructively what it means to consider a human being as a volume. Readers will come across the theoretical elements of the first part. In the fifth part (the third chapter), I will discuss some anthropological and philosophical stances which could resemble a description of or reflection on the human being, and I will consider their opposition or the impossibility to adhere to this anthropological goal. I needed to take into consideration the ways in which a volume is theorized to identify the points that confused me in these anthropological stances and find out what prevents them from radically focusing on the human volume. It is mostly through some approaches of social or cultural anthropology that I want to start a debate, since – besides being the field of study I teach and in which I do my research – it has always displayed a strong empirical interest in the human dimension, while also bypassing it for several theoretical and methodological reasons. It is within this conceptual framework that I prefer referring to, as I will state, existantial[4] anthropology rather than existential anthropology. In fact, it is because I am dissatisfied with the directions of phenomenology and existentialism that I am led in the sixth part (the fourth chapter) to re-read Lévi-Strauss, redefine his anthropological aims and use a structural approach to support and scrutinize the anatomy of volumic unity. I will then confirm the notion of "structural existantism". By way of conclusion and as an opening towards other ways of thinking about the topic, I will suddenly move on to a different field by briefly using the ideas that some artists, specifically Rodin and Giacometti, had about the act of looking. This will allow me to present art as a paradigm for anthropology or as an example that may help it question its way of observing, perceiving and targeting the singularity of beings. These chapters should be read as different expressions of a goal that involves introducing human beings themselves as a topic in anthropology and learning to look at them, describe them and understand them as entities. Some points will become clearer and more complete chapter after chapter. Readers will also find some methodological clarifications and empirical questions that encourage comparative observations.

---

4 The "a" is especially relevant in French since the word *existant* (in French) designates the beings who exist.

The three quotes above, which I used as epigraphs, aptly indicate the content of this book: adopting a new perspective, specifically oriented towards the human being; not separating actions from the whole of which they constitute merely a part; trying to think about the human being and continuing to do so as we realize that he is always replaced by other concerns in anthropology. Looking at a human being, at each human being: this is where I find the anthropologicality of anthropology, its fundamental level and even its essence, if we dare use this word. It seems to me that this first level, that is, human beings, rather than cultures, actions, or relations should be radical, clearly defined and established as the foundations of a discipline, if cross-disciplinary connections are then to be conceived.

This book owes much to my regular conversations with Catherine Beaugrand. We both know what came out of them. I thank her very much. I would also like to thank Étienne Bimbenet, Camille Chamois, Jan Patrick Heiss, Emmanuelle Savignac and Yann Schmitt for reading this book either in part or cover to cover. My discussions with Benoît Haug, Marine Kneubühler, Stefano Montes, Jean-Michel Salanskis, Gwendoline Torterat, Huon Wardle and She Zhenhua allowed me to make some points clearer. I also want to mention my daughters, Manon and Charlotte, who, thanks to their fields of study (philosophy, psychology and biology), regularly helped me in understanding various aspects of the human volume.

Albert PIETTE
February 2019

Introduction

The Common Thread of this Book:
The Anthropological Reversal

1. It may seem at first that the human being, or the individual, has represented and still represents a constant in anthropology. Thus, introducing the human being as a topic into the anthropological field could appear naïve. However, I think that the human being has never really been considered in anthropology. The goal of this book is to conceive the foundations or conditions, both theoretical and methodological, that will allow us to consider the human being as an empirical entity and as a topic for observation and analysis. This book does not concern a specific "field". However, it is not a philosophical book either. It is a book that focuses on theoretical anthropology in the etymological sense of the word: its aim is to present a way of looking at the human being or, as I should say, *a* human being.

2. Despite remaining the main variable and the criterion for fieldwork in anthropological research, culture as a focus has been significantly questioned for quite a few years in favor of action, practices or experience. I am not interested in culture, society, a group, a social class or representations. However, I am also not interested in a situation, a relation or an interaction, with their specific dynamics and rules, or in an action, a practice, an activity or an experience. I do not want to focus on a human being either as part of a group or as he interacts, carries out a specific action, or lives a certain experience and social situation. In their own way, such starting points, such as those based on culture or any other macroentity, are mechanisms that bypass the human being.

2.1. What is going on and what is the issue? What does it mean "to fragment the human unity"? I want to show that, through this operation, this unity is associated with and reduced to a specific dimension, to some kind of partial "in the capacity of" (e.g. carrying out an action, moving, speaking, belonging to a group, having emotions or a subconscious, carrying out a moral action, undergoing a cognitive process) and possibly to specific subjects or specialties in anthropology. Therefore, this operation implies highlighting parts, extracting them from the volumic entity and in a certain way forgetting this entity itself as well as, in some cases, forgetting that it has been forgotten when we think that the "in the capacity of" we choose, for example the social sphere, subjectivity or other dimensions, represents the whole entity. In anthropology, this fragmentation or reduction process often happens alongside another operation: these competences are observed in relations, social situations, social phenomena, social systems, cultural groups and contexts that define the focus of a researcher, guide his approach and often become the explicit themes at the center of the analysis or the topics that the researcher attempts to clarify. In this case, fragmentation is accompanied by a type of dilution of the unity itself, which is placed in groups with other humans. This operation is typical of the social sciences. According to the dictionary, dilution implies a mixture, an attenuation, a decrease in strength and a gradual disappearance. This is exactly what happens. Thus, anthropology is not emancipated from sociological, ethnological or culturological studies. To tell the truth, presenting the human being in relation to other human beings or the environment, in a given social or cultural context, involves simultaneously fragmentation and dilution. In addition, it is often underpinned by the idea that every entity has then been considered, whereas in reality it is merely fragmented and diluted.

2.2. Thus, fulfilling the anthropologicality of anthropology must involve a reversal or an inversion. Using the human volume as central focus is the opposite, on the one hand, of fragmentation, which highlights a fragment or an aspect of the human being (which is then pushed into the background) and, on the other hand, of social contextualization as dilution, which also relegates and subordinates the human being. I do not mean to say that a human being is not part of one group and then of another group, in one situation and then in another situation, or that he does not carry out a series of actions and does not live a series of experiences. This does not mean that an action, a practice and experience leave no traces. Learning to consider a human being and to look "straight" into his existence means learning to separate him from these different frameworks that, according to the interpretations used in the social sciences, prevail over him. Choosing to work on human unity means highlighting this unity and considering that both the different fragmentations into actions, activities, experiences, relations and the different frameworks in a situation, event or society are enabled only because of the presence of entities and whole volumes, as it were. Have we ever seen an action, experience or group without a human entity that carries it out or lives it? The human being is empirically and ontologically necessary for there to be what is the usual focus of the social sciences. Thus, through this reversal, human unity, which is usually relegated to the "background", even in the anthropological tradition, becomes the central "figure", whereas situations, cultures, relations, actions, activities, experiences and environments become secondary. All of this is still there, and it concerns a human being, but it is the human being as unity that represents the observation and comprehension target. Thus, I can rephrase my topic: a human being *who is in interaction*; a human being who is in *interaction*; or *a human being*, who is in interaction (and who is more than that). Interaction may be replaced by relation, action, activity, experience, cultural belonging, etc. Based on the words in italics, we are not considering and thinking about the same thing. In the first two cases, there is a qualification, a restriction imposed immediately by the relative clause. The issue is then to consider the human being as he is in interaction, or even to consider the interaction itself with its rules. In the third case, the relative clause specifies one mode (one of many) of the human being who constitutes the focus. This is the meaning expressed by the comma in the third phrase, which highlights "a human being". Once we focus on several human beings in interaction, it is difficult not to consider the second case, which involves thinking about interactions or relations. In a letter he sent to Henri Fantin-Latour, Édouard Manet mentioned the *Pablo de Valladolid*, a painting by Diego Velázquez that he had seen at the museum in which it was displayed in Madrid: "[It is] the most astonishing piece of painting ever done... the background disappears: it is air which surrounds the fellow, dressed all in black and full of life." After discovering this painting, Manet painted *The Fifer* as a whole human being, seemingly detached from the world. I do not mean to say that the context becomes completely absent, but that it becomes in fact secondary. It appears in a volume himself, as shown by the fifer, while also imposing its presence to the observer. However, when I remove a human being from his connections to other human beings and his contexts, I do not do so to reconsider him at once and mostly alongside other human beings and in specific situations. Contrary to what Merleau-Ponty wrote, I do not take a step back, with the "intentional threads which attach us to the world" in order to bring them to "our notice" [MER 05, p. xv].

3. Thus, I attempt to turn the human being, a human being, into a "field" study like any other entity, be it a city, a religion, hierarchical relations, the psyche, a cell or neuronal connections. No entity, including the human being, is independent of what surrounds it. Just like a city depends on its inhabitants, region and country, so a brain is part of a body, neurons are part of a brain, etc. However, considering an "object" detached from its background and finding a type of singularity is an ordinary scientific operation. Otherwise, each researcher would have had to take into account all of the planet and the whole universe since the dawn of time. This should be all the more simple as the human being represents a perfectly delimited entity from the beginning of his existence to his end and perceiving or structuring this object is not as hard as the examples I have just mentioned, for example a religion, a city or hierarchical relations. Perhaps, the obvious nature of this outline is seen as a trap, and we would reasonably prefer to reduce the human being to an aspect, combine him with other human beings, or mention cultural representations that may disqualify him from being an entity. Yet, this would mean losing what could be, at least etymologically, the object of anthropology, namely the human being. The live and detailed observation of one human being at a time in the continuity of moments represents for me the typical work of an anthropologist, and so does comparing such observations. If we accept that the variety of cultures or social situations is not self-evidently – except for historically and institutionally – the primary object of anthropology, then how can we place this human being as the central focus of a field of research?

3.1. It is here that the answer I suggest comes into play: the "volume". This represents a notion or a concept but also a reality, since a human being is a volume. From an anthropological perspective, I think that this idea is quite powerful and has a more defined heuristic effect than some words that may be related to it, such as "individual", which is occasionally pejorative, ideologically charged and unable to define the consistency of a being itself as clearly, or "person", which is often mixed with interpretations in terms of sociocultural representation or moral issues and the question concerning the criteria that establish when this term should be assigned. Nor would I favor the notion of organism or life, which may correspond to a biological and physiological dimension. I would also say that the body is merely an element of a volume. The notion of existence is widely used in the social sciences and assigned to numerous entities[1]. With the qualifying word "human"[2], the notion of existence, considered in several philosophical senses, may seem too "slippery" and unstable. In any case, I only regard it as the concrete succession of instants. In my opinion, the notion of volume, associated with that of existence, is quite important if we want to identify and adopt an empirical focus on the human being himself while also clarifying this anthropological reversal. To this end, the actual volume, a human being, goes hand in hand with the concept of volume, namely a theoretical representation associated with a set of characteristics that the anthropologist has theorized or, in other words, observed and turned into concepts. The word "volume", which I employ, results then from bringing together what a volume is in common parlance, that is, the fact that a human being is actually a volume and can be recognized as such, and its anthropological explanation. This volume is a volume of being or a human volume. Let us say that it is an anthropological volume. I use these expressions, including the word "volume" on its own, as synonyms.

3.2. Looking at a volume does not mean simply looking in a general way. The goal of the idea of volume is to directly focus on the empirical unity that a human being constitutes in his entirety and that emerges against the background of a context that has become secondary. Considering the human being as a volume may help us "grasp" him, as he tends to slip away and be overlooked. This is a way of "seizing" him. Thus, a volume is separate from all others and can be outlined, in every part of the world, regardless of the ways in which he is represented and perceived. This volume of being thus becomes the observed entity, in his consistency and density together with the components that he expresses or contains, for example an emotion, an action, a word, a thought or a skill. However, in these cases, an anthropologist conceives these as interrelated and as elements of the whole, which are not removed and cannot be separated from the unity of the whole. Presenting and describing a human being as a volume implies integrating at all times these various dimensions (as well as others) without neglecting the volumic unity, as these dimensions represent in most cases, as we have

---

1 For my point of view on the ontological turn, see [PIE 16, pp. 20–25, p. 51 and *sq.*] and [KNE 19]. I think that the requirements of ontology should encourage us to choose how we apply the notion of existence and not to use it broadly, as is the case today in the publications of several anthropologists, and moreover without any focus on the human being.

2 I referred specifically to this point in [PIE 15] and [PIE 16]. The issue is less to reject this notion than to strengthen it because of the idea of volume.

observed, the objects of fragmented analyses. Thus, the goal is to encourage this theoretical approach that has the potential to unify a human being, to regard and consider him as an entity, and, therefore, to identify what I think is the observation and analysis work that needs to be carried out by anthropology. The idea of volume involves a way of looking and discovering. It is in this sense that it is a "theory".

3.3. Introducing the notion of "volume" does not simply involve a way of considering and conceiving a human being. As I have said, this human being is a volume, all of us are one, and we all differ from one another. Altogether, everyone is a volume, whereas partially everyone is merely consciousness, subjectivity, intention, relation and action. This is what a volume indicates, always encouraging us to put aside any perspective that has a specific target. Choosing a type of reading that focuses, for example, on subjectivity or action means neglecting elements that do not correspond to it and which could not fit in this or that particular dimension. A volume always includes other things: what is left by each possible interpretation and even by different combined interpretations.

4. The social sciences, cognitive science, psychology, neuroscience and biology constitute scales or scientific approaches that differ from those employed by the anthropology of volume. The issue faced by the latter is simple: there is a gulf between, on the one hand, the observation and knowledge of volumes considered separately in the continuity of their existence and, on the other hand, the observation and knowledge of individuals considered together or fragmented. It is this gap that anthropology as I intend it should try to bridge in order to fulfill what I think should be its primary role: to be a science that deals with the human being, namely to be a volumology that does not slide him towards these other scales.

4.1. The following words are drawn from a recent article, published in the journal *L'Homme*, which advocates the interrelation of biological and ethnological knowledge in order to pursue a general type of anthropology:

> A fundamental research field, as a general type of anthropology should be, cannot be revitalized by simply searching for new objects: there is significant potential in renewed approaches that take into consideration the technical developments of related fields of study on key topics, such as kinship, body techniques,

communication, cooperation, religions, the imagination, nutrition, or domestication. [BOC 17, p. 240]

I notice that the human being is not mentioned – nor is the living being – as the goal of a general type of anthropology presented as a cross-disciplinary dialog, especially with natural sciences, from the study of social phenomena. This is my finding of this paper: no human beings, and no anthropology as a specific field of study. According to this quote, anthropology is either social[3] or an unequal blend of different types of knowledge. In any case, even if we include what we call "general anthropology", the human being is still bypassed, and actually mixed and fragmented, within and by "societies" and also "environments", which are often considered important in this cross-disciplinary structure. I would like to see a radical anthropology that considers the human being and the entity he constitutes to have its own scale, which differs from that of sociology or biology, and to propose its own terminology, without representing a juxtaposition, integration or unification of different sciences[4]. It is only after such an anthropological stance, which is centered on the human being, studied in depth while remaining separate from "natural" as well as "cultural" sciences, that anthropology could in a second phase proceed to carry out methodologically structured cross-disciplinary operations, for example, in collaboration with neuroscience. I am thinking about a twofold uninterrupted observation, that is, of the human volume, whom I would consider on an anthropological scale, and at the same time of neurons or neuronal connections. In this case, the notion of "biology" would take on a precise meaning that refers to a specific scale[5]. Naturally, it is also possible to adopt prehistoric and evolutionary perspectives[6]. Similarly, comparisons between beings and volumes, whether human or not (rather than merely their activities), which are quite rare, play a significant part in an approach that

3 It may also be called "linguistic" or "biological", but this has no effect on the argument about the status of the human being.

4 Concerning this debate about the "human science" as interrelation of different types of knowledge, we can refer, for example, to François Azouvi's introduction to his book on Maine de Biran [AZO 95]. For some historical and fairly theoretical goals of "human sciences", see [CAR 13].

5 This is not the case in all the arguments – occasionally somewhat vague – concerning the "biological dimension", for example [PAL 13a, p. 40].

6 This is what I did in previous books such as *Anthropologie existentiale* [PIE 09] or *L'Origine de la croyance* [PIE 13a].

aims to understand the human volume. It is important to point out that, on the contrary, present-day "zoocentrism"[7] or "eco-centrism", when they emerge in anthropology through an increasing interest, under different expressions and intellectual affiliations, in "human-animal" relations, ecological issues or "environmental humanities", and more generally in the topic of "non-humans", constitute an additional way of bypassing the human being, following the aforementioned detours.

4.2. What do I mean to say? The human volume is a whole that includes all of his components and a way of structuring. Thus, to consider him properly, we should then avoid losing him in collective phenomena and different relations, by refusing to fragment him in a biological or psychological dimension and turn anthropology into a cross-disciplinary or general discourse. This is to me what anthropology should be. In my opinion, it is very important for anthropology to have its own topic, strictly speaking the human being, and for research to include an indisputable anthropological dimension. However, this is not a plea for a return to an "anthropocentric" paradigm, I mean one centered on the human being in the human and social sciences, given that the human being has never been, as I pointed out, their epistemological center. No epistemological "exceptionalism" has been assigned to the human entity in the history of anthropology which, through its theories, methodologies and topics, has always targeted and continues to target other entities. Rather, the issue is to lay foundations to this end and to create the conditions for a type of anthropology associated with an objective anthropologism. Therefore, it is astonishing to read that the social sciences in the last few years, specifically by highlighting the non-human sphere, have managed to shift their focus away from the human being and that they are experiencing an epistemological revolution through their emphasis on relations. However, the social sciences, sociology or social anthropology, have been deeply relationist in different ways since they were established, as they try to understand and explain individuals with and through other individuals, cultures and interactions. Anthropology could greatly benefit from distancing itself from this approach in order to build an autonomous type of epistemology that makes it possible to refer to the human being as an entity situated at the center and in the foreground, as a volume whom we see continue and live on instant after instant. Unlike what we may think, this type of perspective breaks with a type of epistemology that has always found

---

7 For this critique of zoocentrism, see [BIM 17].

arguments and, as it were, alibis, which were occasionally combined, to avoid focusing on the human being: cultural diversity, social relations, intersubjectivity, the non-human dimension or ecology.

4.2.1. The gap between the volumology that I have just outlined and the monadology put forward by Tarde is equal to the one that may separate anthropology and sociology. Tarde's works significantly emphasize individuals:

> This world would not exist without them; without the world, conversely, the elements would still be something. The attributes which each element possesses in virtue of its incorporation into its regiment do not form the whole of its nature; it has other tendencies and other instincts which come to it from its other regimentations; and, moreover (we will shortly see the necessity of this corollary), still others which come to it from its basic nature, from itself, from its own fundamental substance which is the basis of its struggle against the collective power of which it forms a part. [TAR 12, p. 47]

This last point is especially significant. The complexity of the individual entity ready to move constitutes a strong principle of Tardean sociology: starting from what is small, from details and from differences. However, from this starting point, the explicit "renewed monadology" project [TAR 12, p. 26] turns into a consideration of the "tendency of monads to assemble" [TAR 12, p. 34]. Naturally, there are "men who speak, each with a different accent, intonation, voices, gestures", but this heterogeneity gives rise to habits, associations and rules whose social laws about imitation, transmission and propagation should be sought, according to Tarde. Therefore, through their active force and their eagerness, monads constitute indispensable means which, however, should be employed to consider mutual ownership as well as power and resistance relations. Thus, activity, action and relation re-emerge as objects at the center of this sociological analysis. Finally, society is regarded as a "mental communion", which is certainly imperfect, or as a "web of inter-spiritual actions and mental states affecting one another" [TAR 02, p. 11]. In short, a theoretical approach to relation, connection and association, such as we can see it in Bruno Latour's work, which often acknowledges its Tardean inspiration, seems to have replaced the way of conceiving the entire volume as observed now and instant after instant. Thus, the shift involved in the volumological principle seems radical to me.

4.2.2. I would like to clarify something. We may say that a human being is quite negligible when compared with the planet and the time of the universe. This is true. However, he represents the topic on which anthropology focuses. Aiming to describe the human being does not correspond specifically to a humanistic perspective, but it is an anthropological act that does not imply that the human being should be considered as a "wonder" or "the wonder of wonders", as Groethuysen claims when he presents Ficino and Pico della Mirandola's philosophy [GRO 80, p. 150]. Besides, I would like to acknowledge that there is a touch of pathos in a type of anthropology that describes fleeting individuals. Let us say that there are at least four reasons why anthropology should learn to develop its interest in human beings or, better, in human volumes. We could first consider the range of evolutionary change, over several hundred thousand years, which assigned to humans the place and role we know. What happened to the human being then? This question is enough to justify compared observations of volumes, including other similar species. Furthermore, the evolutionary specificities of the human being could encourage anthropology to focus on "individuals" and describe them as directly concerned by the succession of instants following one another. These individuals are especially concerned since, based on complex learning, memorization and linguistic processes, humans are like "extreme individuals" [PRO 12, p. 148], each of them attached in a specific manner to their individuality and aware that as time passes they inch closer to their disappearance. Naturally, this has nothing to do with a contemporary kind of individualism. Then, it is easy to see that in most cases humans have so-called feelings of friendship and love towards other human beings which, with very few exceptions, they do not feel towards other species. Everyone, indeed, pairs with his or her own "fellows". A science called anthropology and practiced by humans is interested directly in the human being and seems self-evident. Moreover, human beings are also the ones who hurt other humans the most and who wound, murder and carry out atrocious acts that seem intolerable, unacceptable and unbearable to most other beings. This may lead us to think that there are (more) things to learn and consider about humans or, better, to understand in detail about these volumes.

5. This book will constantly deal with "volumes". Readers will come across the points mentioned in this introduction and find, now and again,

volumes as seen from various perspectives. With anthropological reversal as a goal, considering the human being as a volume involves at least three significant actions: focusing on the volumic entity in its unity and continuity; understanding the volume himself first and not based on others, the context, or the external origin of the elements that constitute him; and paying heed to the details of the volume, and more specifically to the leftovers forgotten by other types of interpretations. This assigns a great descriptive role to anthropology. The notions and concepts I suggest are in line with this goal, namely observing and grasping a human being, the volume observed by an anthropologist, as closely and precisely as possible. Based on this focus on the human being, I move on to what may seem a completely different topic. Luke Howard, at the beginning of the 19th Century, gave different names to clouds – cumulus and stratus clouds, cirrus and nimbus clouds – so that we can now observe and recognize them. He spelled out their shapes, appearances and structure; their ability to change and grow bigger or smaller; their density and density variations; their altitude, their expansion and retraction degree; as well as their indetermination, transition and their dynamic between stability and change. I want to keep in mind this extraction through which Howard created an object, clouds in their own right, while removing them from all the elements moving across the sky [WEB 16]. Goethe, who commented on Howard, wrote keeping in mind "morphology" as a goal:

> The man of science has always evinced a tendency to recognize living forms as such, to understand their outwardly visible and tangible parts in relation to one another, to lay hold of them as indicia of the inner parts, and thus, in contemplation, to acquire a degree of mastery over the whole. [GOE 52, p. 88]

Theory: Observing the Human Volume

What do we see when we look at a human volume? Just as it represents an act of looking, theory is a discovery, an analysis, but also a question. This part, the theory of the volume, includes five sections that describe the anthropological volume: as a consistency with the different elements that constitute him, and on whom these elements simultaneously depend; as an entirety to be grasped in his "extremities" and details; as an individual and singular unity that is separate from the others and attempts to establish relations; as a continuity that remains stable beyond microvariations as time goes by; but also as an entity that acts, feels and simultaneously lessens what happens. These are actually five different starting points, which represent each a way of looking at and understanding a volume. They provide different pieces of information about a volume, but they also respond to, complete, and interact with one another, besides recurring at times. Undoubtedly, it would be better to follow the progression I suggest, but readers may also read the sections included in this part in any order they choose. I will begin a dialog with some anthropologists, but it is mostly in one of the following sections that this will take place.

1.1. Volume and voluments

1. The word "volume" has an interesting lexical range. It is quite revealing as a way of helping us watch or observe. A volume is first of all a "scroll of parchment or papyrus containing written matter", all the sheets gathered together by binding, "a single book or collection of printed sheets", a book [OXF 10]. Scrolling, winding and binding indicate some ways of keeping a volume together and making it a unity. Loose sheets, bound sheets

and texts are the contents of a volume. Just as there are no books without these elements and as these elements become meaningful only when contained in a book, there can be no volumes without the components that constitute them and which themselves need to be contained in a volume to exist. Moreover, according to the etymology of the word "volume", the verb *volvere* indicates a movement and certain actions: rolling, causing to roll, letting time go by, but also stirring something in one's heart and meditating in one's mind. As a three-dimensional solid, a human volume moves, is situated in time and follows variable rhythms. A volume can also be measured. This reveals that it is possible to conceive different intensities, strengths or ranges in relation to the components of the human volume. However, beyond these variations, he remains the same continuing unity that can be perceived and recognized. Thus, observing a human volume means looking at an envelope with contents, but also at an entity with a certain consistency, namely a concrete entirety whose coherence is ensured by voluments contained in the volume and a certain resistance to change.

1.1. While comparing animal with vegetal forms, Francis Hallé refers to their potential characteristics in terms of area and volume. Thus, he pits plants, which "in spite of [their] modest volume, must produce huge subterranean and aerial surface" [HAL 02, p. 44] against animals, which are "essentially volumes covered by small external surfaces" [HAL 02, p. 47]. Biologists, who consider this feature an important element for their understanding of the different ways in which energy is captured, even point out that "the double requirement of finding prey and avoiding becoming prey to others" constitutes "powerful constraints, promoting the evolution of animals that optimize their volumes" since "their mobility increases with size, up to a limit" [HAL 02, p. 47]. Thus, we can see that a human volume includes solid, liquid and gaseous elements that can be of interest to biologists or other scientists. However, anthropologists focus on other components, that is, those related to the anthropological volume. We also know that the anthropology of the volumes does not wish to fragment them, to reduce them to specific parts or to dilute them in a situation or a culture. It is a matter of striking a balance between these two issues: considering a volume and simultaneously, inevitably, a certain number of his components. Which of these elements can be found in the anthropological volume?

1.2. I use the word "voluments", which is a portmanteau of element and volume, to refer to the visible or invisible elements that concern the anthropology of the volume. The word "volument" indicates that these elements belong to and are situated within a volume, that they are carried and expressed by him and that they could not exist outside his entity. There are several of them, that is, actions, gestures, words, the body, a body posture, thoughts, mental images, reasons (for action), perceptions, sensations, feelings, affects, emotions, desires, wishes, intentions, moods, memories, values, cognitive abilities[1], types of consciousness, knowledge, know-hows, so-called social and cultural characteristics[2], various memberships and roles[3], different habits or style[4]. This list is not necessarily exhaustive[5]. These voluments – for example, a gesture, a thought, or a disposition – are quite different in their modes of expression, degree of variability or place occupied in a volume. In any case, each volument is expressed in a specific manner: it is a singular action, gesture, knowledge, thought or habit of this or that volume[6]. Not all of them manifest themselves at each moment or in every situation. Some, like social dispositions or a stylistic expression, have long been anchored in a volume with their specific aspects, and they cannot really be prevented from expressing themselves alongside other voluments; some types of knowledge or reasons for action may be active just as they remain implicit; specific ideas or memories may also have been stable and yet take shape more intermittently. Other voluments, for example, a thought, a gesture or an emotion, can be expressed in many more ways, sometimes even ephemerally or sporadically, than habits or style. As I have pointed out, many voluments may have variable

1 They may also refer to, for example, reasoning, doubting and taking distance.

2 By social characteristics or traces I mean those that directly indicate social "classes" and family "trajectories". Cultural traces derive from being exposed to specific practices or ways of thinking in larger areas.

3 A role, which may also be understood in the sense of an activity, is what becomes activated in a situation, with the know-hows and knowledge, awareness of rules or norms, values, or mental scripts of a volume. It may be found in actions characterized by habits. It can also be supplemented by a feeling of duty, unease, or responsibility, or insincere thoughts.

4 I single out personal style as the result of different experiences and situations which, however, cannot be integrated into the outline of so-called social trajectories and cultural marks. I will broadly define the style as: "a recurrent way of behaving and acting in life which is strictly characteristic and singular to a person".

5 Each of these voluments could be discussed in depth and become the object of entire studies, whether empirical or theoretical. As I mention them here in their common meaning, that is, the one given in dictionaries, I will necessarily frustrate experts in voluments, in particular cognitivists, dispositionalists, psychoanalysts and interactionists, be they anthropologists, psychologists or sociologists.

6 Thus, for example, know-hows may be more or less specialized or general. For instance, they may involve driving a car but also recognizing some situations and take on a specific role according to well-known rules. The overall knowledge of a volume may concern an infinite number of general or specialized branches.

degrees of intensity and increase or decrease in expression, emotion, tension or weight perceived in a volume, who seems to fill up and become empty.

1.2.1. These voluments, understood as such and not in relation to a causal explanation of a biological, physical or chemical kind, which I will not describe by "delving" into, for example, the neuronal or muscular structure, in order to keep the focus on the anthropological scale specifically, are necessary for anthropologists. Volume helps us "grasp" the human being, as I said, but how can observers keep a volume in mind and consider him properly, once they have grasped him, if not based on his voluments? This is the goal of voluments such as I have considered them, without here aiming to define the human being. How can he be described and explained with precision on his own scale if not through what may appear at the surface of the volume, that is, visible voluments (actions, gestures), as Goethe wrote, and also through what he contains, that is voluments (feelings, knowledge) which sometimes leave visible traces? When they do not leave visible traces – such as in the cases of mental images or thoughts – they are not for that reason inaccessible. By taking into consideration all these voluments, without any privileged focus, an anthropologist will try not to lose the unity of a volume based on a good amount of details but without the micrological itemization and punctiliousness employed by an expert in cognitive tasks or motion physiology. This can be done because of a type of observation that, while obviously careful, can still be carried out by anthropologists with their specific knowledge and competences. Therefore, the anthropological volume does not include any brain or neurons, muscles, atoms, molecules, cells or genes. However, as I pointed out in the introduction, there is no reason why the scale considered here could not be occasionally and meticulously complemented and supplemented with and by observations based on other scales – in this case, in necessary collaboration with researchers in the fields of study concerned, in particular biology and neuroscience. This gives me the opportunity to point out that, in an anthropological volume, the voluments included in the aforementioned list may appear as "universals" or, in any case, as general enough to be present or potentially present in every human being.

1.2.2. Can we imagine a volume at a given time t with only one volument activated, that is, an action, gesture, perception, thought, style, social mark, or any other volument? No, we cannot. However, several descriptions (or theories) proceed as if only one, two or three voluments were concerned – this is what the fragmentation process involves. Several voluments simultaneously complement, nuance and complete one another. They create the density of a volume. For example, drinking a glass of cola in my kitchen constitutes a moment of presence that activates several voluments. It includes at least a more or less strong intention linked to the previous instants, the desire to drink, the knowledge that there is some cola and a glass in a specific place, the skill involved in opening the bottle, a gesture a personal style that can be seen in the fact that I feel like drinking cola, in my way of holding the glass, in my mood, for example if I am happy, and also in my thoughts about the work that has been carried out, and maybe also in a bodily perception or feeling. I would say that all these voluments are "compresent" with the action of drinking. Thus, "compresence" defines a combination and articulation of voluments at a given time t. In another situation, a specific role may become involved with its own rules and regulate my way of holding the glass or drinking, as well as my mood and thoughts. At another time, giving money to someone begging in the subway involves an association over a few instants of a perception of poverty, a feeling (e.g. of sympathy), a desire to give concrete shape to a value and to a carefully considered thought about this action, as all of these aspects create an act that is qualified as moral. Yet, I am interested less in the action than in the volume with his voluments, whose gesture and affect in question are pervaded by a specific style or social habit, combined with a particular mood or thought as the action is carried out, accompanied by the memory of an old traumatic event, and soon followed by other gestures that correspond to another situation and another moment, which may retain the thought of the previous moral act or take shape alongside different thoughts and so on. Thus, there are numerous examples of the compresence of voluments based on their diversity and variable combinations, which let each or some of them become more or less significant according to the moment.

1.2.2.1. In a moment of presence, it is possible to retrieve some types of compresence of relations between voluments. These relations may be:

– A causality or a chain of voluments, for example, when a desire, an intention or a thought sets off an action that generates another feeling and so on, based on interrelated series of actions in a more or less automatic or conscious manner.

– A concretization, when a specific know-how, which could not take shape otherwise, is expressed in a precise action or specific gesture, or when a role is fulfilled, according to the representation of this role or to a value deemed important. I could also say that such an action requires a specific type of knowledge or that such a thought requires a rational ability.

– A simultaneity when an action is carried out together with another action, which is completely unrelated to the former or with a thought, various images that distract it, or a mood or emotion that may have nothing to do with the act itself but may intensify, disrupt or pervade it. It is also the case when this action and its awareness create more or less strong tensions with ideas, memories, types of knowledge, values or a firmly anchored social or cultural mark; but also when a specific stylistic trait or social mark are well suited or do not "tally with" the role about to be fulfilled.

– A "direction" when, for example, a feeling is about the body, a gesture, an action in progress or a cultural affiliation, so that, for example, these are felt as a constraint; when a specific word is immediately the object of self-derision, when thinking concerns the action in course or past emotions; when our consciousness focuses explicitly on a specific gesture, role, social characteristic or stylistic trait and, otherwise, when there are no bodily feelings or perceptions, or even no (or no extant) memories of events that have been buried.

– A permeation when a gesture, word or body posture is pervaded by a style, a social or cultural habit, or a role with the knowledge and know-how it implies and the actions it involves. These are pervading voluments. They mark and characterize. Emotions, affects and perceptions can blend with the style and habits to mark an action, a thought or a body posture. These voluments can take on different shapes, but they mainly remain marked by stylistic traits or sociocultural habits.

These compresences can add up; for example, the same action accompanied by a know-how marked itself by a style and involving the perception of a gesture may occur simultaneously with another movement. Thus, it is in this sense that a moment of presence implies bringing together voluments in a volume whom cannot then be reduced to the action itself. I will reiterate that the compresence of voluments does not imply that *all* voluments are activated in an automatic sequence. Besides, some are activated only for a brief moment, for example, a gesture or a word that has no consequence on the other voluments and the following instants.

1.2.2.2. Such are the anthropological volume and the scale on which anthropologists could work. Thus, to seize a moment of presence without resorting to neuronal connections or muscles, one should first indicate the voluments concerned and interweaved in a volume. If I refer to the brief description above about the act of drinking, I obtain: VOLUME AP (at a specific hour, on a specific day, in a specific place) = intention + desire + knowledge + know-how + gesture + style + mood + thought + perception + body. A description should then mention the content or specific expression of the voluments as well as their intensities as they surface or are felt, and identify the different (+) that indicate their dynamics, together with their causality, concretization, permeation, simultaneity and direction. Second, it is also important to mention the consistency[7] of a volumic entity, which does not actually represent a sum, as a volume predates these voluments and their activation. Besides, after their activation, the volume will remain the same or almost the same, even when, in the following instant, some other voluments will become involved. This is also true because there are always some leftover elements that can be retrieved and other potential voluments that have not been activated and do not manifest themselves in this moment and in the "addition" in question. There are other elements remaining, and I could nearly say that there is also some empty space in the volume, which leaves room for other voluments and other manifestations of voluments. Thus, I would like to draw attention to this point: descriptions often run the risk of strongly favoring actions and neglecting volumes, as if the series of verbs threatened to overshadow the consistency and continuity of the volume who accomplishes them. The issue is to attach more importance again to the substantive rather than verbs, revealing what constitutes a volume: in particular, the simultaneity of various voluments, namely the inner, gestural and stylistic density of a volume, his different abilities, not all of which can be mobilized, implicit know-how, accumulated roles, and those aspects that remain the same instant after instant. A volume is a volume of being with his consistency, his continuity and that of his voluments, even before carrying out a specific action and coming from another situation, containing within him these various well-established voluments, types of knowledge, stylistic expressions, habits, ideas, memories, etc. This volume will be changed by the actions he carries out or the emotion he feels at a specific moment, but only negligibly so, if we consider the consistency–continuity that characterizes him. Thus, it is important to emphasize (hence the capital

---

7 Should we point out that readings that adopt approaches based on consistency or stability follow a "highly" Western metaphysics? However, this does not preclude the objective reality of this consistency and the significant role it plays in understanding a human volume. One of the leitmotifs of this book is to take this consistency seriously from an empirical perspective.

letters) the volume identified, especially if we have to describe a series of his acts, with other gestures and thoughts but the same style, body and possibly the same mood. The issue is then to define a volume and his unity beyond his actions and other voluments of his, and to establish clearly his place in relation to these aspects, which become secondary.

1.2.2.3. Voluments cannot be organized outside the volume who carries them. It could not be otherwise. Paying attention to the empirical reality of a volume with his voluments does not mean considering a specific volument, let alone regarding voluments as elements extracted from the volume, or taking into account mainly the ways in which people may imagine and represent – for example, culturally – their own unity or singularity, their relations to other beings, or their ability, in the name of religious ideas, to go out of their volume. This is often interesting for ethnologists, who then stop focusing on the human being himself. "Indigenous knowledge", classification systems about beings in general, ideas or representations about the person may indeed lead in specific circumstances to certain feelings and types of perceptions, but these belong to a volume on whom they depend. As we know, anthropology has often put, and is now putting again, a lot of emphasis on the bias of ethnocentric categories and some opposites (nature–culture, human–non human, for example) established in Western philosophy. Regarding a human being as a volumic entity allows us to consider him besides or before taking into consideration these categories or cultural representations. In order to make use of them and think that we are not human beings or that a stone is a person, we need to be this anthropological volume made up of several voluments. Moreover, within a volume, these categories are not isolated but mobilized in the compresence of other voluments, as they blunt, dull and distance them. Whether humanbeings consider themselves as volumes or not, whether they think that they are collectively interdependent with other human beings or not, or whether they feel they are volumes or not, they still need in any case to be separate entities with a specific consistency. Otherwise, how could they think, feel and act? Voluments, and so ideas, cultural representations or feelings, do not exist outside the specific volume they define and whose components or aspects they represent. It is due to the presence of a volume that voluments can remain the same, change or have consequences, while they characterize this volume.

1.2.3. Overall, this argument allows us to point out a significant element, which may seem evident to some but not necessarily to others. In a volume, there is no "I". It may be at most an effect, occasionally felt, of voluments bouncing off one another: the linguistic possibility of saying I, me or mine with a specific name and surname; a type of attachment to one's own volume; desires perceived as bodily desires or thoughts of one's acts as one's own; different degrees of consciousness, pre-reflexive or reflexive, of a type of continuity; the memory and knowledge of one's past acts; or stylistic fixations, for example – but not only – postural, specific to each volume.

1.2. The entirety of a volume and the density of presence

1. Marked by his consistency, a volume is then an entity made up of different voluments. He is also an entirety. Here, I want to give full meaning to this word. As a visible surface that contains less visible elements, a volume is an intensive entirety with his depth and an extensive entirety with his surface. The role of anthropologists is to attempt to "cover" the container and the inside of a volume, this entirety, by looking for as many voluments as possible and identifying the details of this twofold dimension. The entirety of a volume, explored in full, also concerns his "extremities", namely his feelings, as well as seemingly unimportant details, secondary gestures or fleeting thoughts. These extremities as such reveal in their own way that they belong to the volume in question. They are part of the volume. Their description would be an "extremic description". This is clearly a horizon and a goal that we should constantly try to reach.

1.1. The idea of entirety may recall the notion of totality, which is employed in philosophy and anthropology. However, its meaning or scope seems different to me. For example, Plessner, who rejects "the isolating techniques of psychological and physiological methodology" [PLE 70, p. 16], values the "man as a whole", and not in relation to "some particular aspect which can be detached from the whole in quasi-independent fashion, like body, soul, mind, or social unit" [PLE 70, p. 21]. What a volume encourages us to do is slightly different. Observing a volume naturally does not involve juxtaposing types of knowledge that derive from different fields of study, but considering also and in detail specific elements, that is, voluments, which are compresent in different ways in the volumic unity, without, however, extracting them from it and losing this unity. When Sartre considers individuals as a "totality" in *Being and Nothingness*, he does not regard them as "an addition or by an organization of the diverse tendencies which we have empirically discovered in him" [SAR 56, p. 563]. On the contrary, according to him "in each inclination, in each tendency the person expresses himself completely [SAR 56, p. 563]. Besides, Sartre points out that "it is a matter of rediscovering under the partial and incomplete aspects of the subject the veritable concreteness which can be only the totality of his impulse towards being" [SAR 56, p. 563]. Project of being and totality of being become interlinked in classically Sartrean leitmotifs like "desire of being", "desire of a way of being" and "choice of being". As he writes: "this project itself inasmuch as it is the totality of my being, expresses my original choice in particular circumstances" [SAR 56, p. 564]. When we consider a human being, we see a whole. However, when our aim is to describe, we also turn to his elements and to the voluments of the volume, looking closer without forgetting that they are part of this whole. Thus, based on this volume, the issue is not to adopt a line of thinking where a totality is that which can manifest itself in an attitude, gesture or thought. On the contrary, we have to consider, just as I have pointed out, a unity, that is, the volume, that should be covered as a whole, both superficially and in depth, and identify as many voluments and various elements as possible, including insignificant details. It is with the leftovers and the leftovers of the leftovers added to what is important and seems the salient aspect of the situation that a volume can be properly considered in his presence and movement. In so doing, we can see – as I will mention again – that a volume, who is an entirety, does not express a such a Sartrean totality in his acts. Indeed, the style, as a volument among others, may characterize him and pervade some but not each of these voluments, and it contains various expressions that are not necessarily present in each moment and could not be reasonably associated with a "choice" of being on an empirical level.

1.2. In the history of anthropology, Marcel Mauss undoubtedly represents the most famous example of the idea of totality. He used it on several levels but without specifically targeting the human being. The difference with the volumic entirety on which I focus seems important to me. Mauss first turns anthropology into "the sum of the sciences that consider the human as a living being who is conscious and sociable" [MAU 50, p. 285]. Presented in these terms, a goal of this kind, which has been already mentioned above, becomes the aim of a type of anthropology that has become a cross-disciplinary summary rather than a field of study in itself. In my opinion, this remains a crucial question. From this perspective, Mauss mentions a "total psycho-physiological complex" which interests the "sociologist" such as Maus qualifies himself. He explains that "total" humans can be found especially in "the least developed forms of social life", which are less able to control their conscience and therefore affected by the "least mental shock" [MAU 50, p. 306][8]. This is what would encourage sociologists to collaborate with experts in other fields, especially psychology, in order to carry out better analyses. When Mauss is himself interested in a person, he analyzes more the "notion, the concept that humans from different ages have created for themselves" [MAU 50, p. 335] than their internal complexity. His goal is "a catalog of forms that the notion has taken on at different points" [MAU 50, p. 334]. As Mauss specifies, "what I want to show is the series of forms that this concept has assumed in the life of men in societies, according to their systems of law, their religions, their customs, their social structures and their modes of thought" [MAU 50, p. 335]. A substantial amount of research in social and cultural anthropology follows this avenue as it values discourses and representations. As a last point, Mauss seems to me to be more at ease with the "total social fact", for example about an event that incorporates different aspects which may be legal, economic, religious or aesthetical, with more or less significant weights or ramifications, as they relate to various contexts and entail a number of consequences [MAU 50, p. 274 and ff.]. However, the issue then no longer concerns voluments as parts, strictly speaking, of a volume of being. We have lost the human unity, which is presented as assembled with others and as the expression of a culture, leading Marc Augé to claim that "the individuality he [Mauss] considers is one that represents the culture, a typical individuality" [AUG 09, p. 21]. This encapsulates the entire issue. In contrast, a volumist observation focuses on the entity itself until its very extremity.

2. In order to grasp the extremities of this volumic entirety, I believe that we need to make the observation–description work effective and find supplementary levers for it. The compresence of voluments, as we have seen above, is only a possible way of zooming in or a step. Voluments help us grasp a volume, but we also need to grasp these voluments as far as his extremities. Before their observation or afterwards with the aim of providing a description, according to their way of working, anthropologists need a good net, like a fishing net, to catch and collect as many voluments as possible, both extensively and intensively, while also trying to keep them together without losing the consistency of the volume. It is based on this goal to grasp the entirety of the volume in order to avoid reducing him to a

8 Mauss has suggested a more nuanced way of thinking about "individual character"; for example, succinctly in a conference, see [MAU 04].

role, action, cognition or affect that I suggest four parameters or criteria, each with its respective opposite, bringing together several voluments, whether gestures, perceptions, emotions, know-hows or traces of social trajectories or styles. With these parameters, which cannot be conceived separately, the issue is less to target modes of presence than the presence of a volume and his density. Together and in their double polarity – I emphasize this point – these parameters allow us to describe at a given instant the thickness or the density of the presence of a volume with his comprement voluments in his details and as far as his extremities. They also help us retrieve variable intensities, with simultaneous ways of engaging and disengaging or being active and passive, according to the voluments in question and their relations[9]. Here are the four parameters, based on four opposites whose first terms may indicate ways of emptying a volume or types of disintensity (which I will refer to later on in my discussion of lessereity) and whose second terms may define ways of filling a volume or types of intensity.

– Parsimony corresponds to a routine and alleviated deployment of actions, thoughts and words thanks to well-established habits, know-hows, roles and mental scenarios. It also involves not trying to find out, verify and determine the effects and consequences of one's own or others' intentions or motivations as well as what everyone does with others. The opposite of parsimony is "work", that is, an assessment through a strategy or justification and a focus on responsibility, which mobilize attention, emotion or reflection about specific aspects of reality. In some situations, this may also involve effort or suffering, but these or other forms of intensity can still rely on several external supports and the volume's own style.

– Docility, which is also associated with several habits, types of knowledge, values and reasons to be here, involves abiding by the rules and points of reference of a situation as well as what they naturally encourage us to do. It also involves accepting some voluments that characterize a volume, especially a role, his style or some of their manifestations. Docility means avoiding the challenge of change and the ensuing cognitive, emotional or moral tension. Its opposite is a wish or desire for change, with controversies and challenges. The style of the volume may lead him to be docile or non-docile towards this or that aspect of a situation. In both cases, a volume

---

9 In *Existence in the Details*, I attempted to measure some engagement intensities in moments of presence, assigning numerical values to these parameters [PIE 15, pp. 81–86].

relies on his stylistic tendencies, but in the second case (non-docility) this does not imply that the volume cannot, for example, feel some type of tension.

– Fluidity corresponds to accepting contradictions felt in one's own volume, for example, between different values and roles, or contradictions in a situation. It is fluidity that allows a more or less easy shift between situations, beyond and despite any possible emotion or moral tensions when faced with contradictions and the different issues that the ensuing moments mobilize. Its opposite is inflexibility, that is, refusal to continue and intolerance when faced with the intensity of these tensions. Styles, types of knowledge and know-hows constitute possible supports in both cases.

– Distraction, as it is understood here, corresponds to the ability to consider a being, object or event as a detail (as non-relevant) and turn them into elements that are only slightly distracting, without compromising the minimum attention required by the situation. Thus, distraction implies gestures that are peripheral to a main action, fleeting thoughts which do not represent a burden, and also some expressions of detachment. The opposite of such a distraction is a state of obsession, concentration or alertness.

3. Thinking in these terms about entirety and extremity can shed light on other readings. Above all, it demonstrates an interpretation based not on actions – which would be more restrictive in that it would overlook the density of a volume – but on presence to the extent that it concerns the detailed entirety of a human being at a specific moment. This is a key point in the theory of the volume that attempts to determine the complex density of presence. In fact, what can we observe? At a given time t or for a few seconds, all the parameters in question can mix but also nuance one another. Thus, at this moment, a volume carries out in his parsimony some gestures with objects to which he is accustomed because of a know-how he has mastered, while also being pervaded by a deep emotion related to an old memory or feeling, in a tense mood, a desire to change something in his surroundings – which does not prevent him from being distracted by a noise outside and remember something about the previous day. Another volume, perceiving a strong emotion when confronted with a significant change imposed on him, keeps relying on his habits and accepting the contradictions between the voluments of his volume and those of the present situation. Yet another may decide now, when he feels this tension, to change some elements (values or roles) that he deems contradictory in his existence, as he

has breakfast or listens absent-mindedly to the news on the radio, and then to remain focused on another activity and stop thinking about these contradictions, but then thinking about them again shortly after. If he changes, not without some emotion, a volument of his volume, he keeps relying on other past experiences and routines that govern his activities. The very style of the volume or some of his expressions, as we will say, can often be recognized in his moods or emotions, but also in his desire and decision to change, as well as in his way of achieving this. A volume may even then rely on his own style. This style may favor one of the two poles of the parameters but also differences in intensity of the activated voluments without, however, effacing the presence of the other pole, according to the moment and what may happen in a situation. Let us also point out that docility may involve a strong feeling of boredom and non-docility may be associated with a joyous feeling for a specific volume but not for another. Such moments can be found in everyone's existence. In the continuity of time, no instant can avoid the nuanced density of simultaneity. Thus, describing the extremities of a volume aims to portray this density in the details of the entire volume.

3.1. The interpretation I suggest does not follow the logic of action but targets presences, with their simultaneous and non-exclusive characteristics, trying to cover as much as possible the entirety of the volume. Several theories only concern a specific trait of the eight that have been put forward, losing part of the density of presence. Some theoretical arguments employed in a Bourdieusian approach – and by many other authors – could undoubtedly correspond to parsimony, that is, routines, our practical sense, and the "self-evidence" of ordinary experience. Bourdieu associates this with a "total and unconditional" investment [BOU 90, p. 67]. Presence in a situation also includes a way of being distracted and, to different degrees, an emotion, a mood or even a way of thinking or tense thoughts. All these aspects make this investment less total and unconditional. On the contrary, several action theories highlight the work of meaning and assessment, namely the opposite of parsimony. This is a fairly marked trend in interactionism, ethnomethodology or pragmatic sociology, among other intellectual sources which can also be found in the anthropological tradition and whose theoretical filters as well as research topics favor in most cases interpretations based on assessment, negotiation, justification or interaction, as if the presence linked to the collective issues of the situation were "labor" or an "ordeal"[10]. Thus, a type of terminology is chosen. However, undoubtedly even for the authors of the aforementioned theories, clearly and nearly at every instant and in all situations whatsoever there is nothing of this sort in the reality of a volume, who always finds familiar supports on which he can rely with ease, even as he assesses, informs, lives his emotion, etc. This allows a certain amount of parsimony, some detachment and some distraction to seep in, and this makes it possible to increase in the description the density of the volume. All these remarks tend whether we like it or not to make the theoretical arguments used in several kinds of action sociology or anthropology, which focus on the stakes of the situation and communication pertinence, less "exact" or, in other words, less in keeping with reality, less correct and precise if we refer to the meaning given in dictionaries. The meticulous observation of a volume and his voluments at a given time t, and all the more so in the series of moments following one another, reveals that the possibility of being exclusively active (which implies attention, thinking, will, responsibility, emotion, tension) is as extreme, not to say anthropologically impossible, as the possibility of being exclusively passive, resting on the various habits, beings and objects involved in the situation, accepting things and being slightly distracted[11]. To identify with precision how full and dense a volume is at a given time, it is then important to incorporate properly the part that involves the fact of being active and the part that involves the fact of being passive, considering the most complete diversity of voluments, their types of compresences and their nuanced expressions.

3.2. We can also observe that the central leitmotif of a theory corresponds to a form of feeling at a specific instant in a given situation. This moment and this situation are then lived as a constraint or a type of freedom or a strategy or a deliberate act or an ordeal. For example, we can observe a volume as he regards a specific series of actions as difficult. He perceives it as the need to put on a good face, as Goffman could say. Shortly afterwards, this volume may have different feelings, but in that very moment what is

---

10 A terminology of this kind is clearly defined by Goffman [GOF 67] and Garfinkel [GAR 67] but also by Boltanski-Thévenot [BOL 91] and Latour [LAT 87]. Goffman refers to "joint ceremonial labor" [GOF 67, p. 85]. It is especially significant to see how he re-appropriates the role distance in the logic of role, meaning, and pertinence. see [PIE 15, p. 32 and ff.]. It is also in this category that I would put, for example, the works carried out by Jeanne Favret-Saada.

11 For mixed presence, see [PIE 15, pp. 555–558, 68–90]. See also, based on a different problem, [HEI 15a, pp. 238–262].

there in addition to this? There are always other things that nuance the feeling of constraint or tension, as if that feeling could not be total and manifest itself in full, since various supports and points of reference are there, preventing the feeling in question from being stronger. These nuances facilitate the chain and the continuity between situations. It is in this context that it may be important to retrieve those details and feelings that do not seem to directly concern the action and the main role: an evasive look, temporary distractions, fleeting thoughts, anticipations of following moments, or the traces of past moments. Thus, in order to describe a moment, I think that it is not sufficient to accumulate, even on a simultaneous level, logics of action or the corresponding perceptions, which are classically identified in the social sciences (strategy, rationality, criticism, invention, as well as others). They should also be supplemented by some leftovers and various details, which are not necessarily indicated by these logics of action[12]. The reality of a volume imposes the details and nuances of its presence on each "as if" of theory, which reveals a specific characteristic of the human being, like an actor playing a part, like a rational being or a strategist, as well as on the added "as ifs". All the aforementioned parameters may make it possible to incorporate these different logics of action and add to them some leftovers.

4. I will dig out from the anthropological tradition itself two recent theoretical proposals in order to compare them with the requirements entailed by the volumic entirety principle. For example, while Maurice Bloch is right in his attempt to show how anthropology has always found it difficult to consider the inner complexity of an individual and has preferred the study of the discursive representations and categorizations [BLO 12, Chapter 6], his cognitive anthropology, in my opinion, seems to limit the human volume, called "blob". This blob is presented together with its various levels of consciousness (thus, the feeling of having a body, being the author of one's actions, a temporal continuity and also a narrative ability) and a "social and communicative aspect", which "links up and, to a certain extent, merges different but nonetheless distinct blobs, different people linked by social ties, in other words", as M. Bloch writes [BLO 12, p. 140]. A blob is actually "an ever-modifying locus of reception and emission of an extraordinary number of messages which we and others transform, merge and remake within the environment in which we live" [BLO 12, p. 34].

---

12 Elsewhere, I have mentioned some possible interpretations based on simultaneous logics of action: [PIE 13b, pp. 62–65, PIE 15].

Then, the task of anthropologists involves above all grasping "the flow of mental concepts and schema and of mind reading that occurs in social situations" [BLO 12, p. 180], and thus focusing on the relevance of what constitutes the collective relevance. Ultimately, the blob appears to be a cognition, learning and memory pole, and thus it is only a part of a volume of reduced density. In any case, the blob can be used as a lever to consider and theorize the volume; it implies at first, at the beginning of the research, favoring specific voluments and putting others aside, especially, but not exclusively, many feelings which require specific types of introspection to be expressed. Social anthropology is not used to this, as it is interested in particular in the implicit aspects of the social exchange per se, a point which Maurice Bloch discusses at length. Thus, the blob is associated not only with cognition but also with the social situation, communication and exchange, indeed in relation to the diversity of cultures. One of the key principles in the idea of volume is in fact not to involve a type of observation that is too targeted and dominated by the collective issue related to a situation. The focus remains on the volume, and his presence almost necessarily clashes with another theoretical proposal, in this case analyses based on types, regimes or other classificatory frameworks. There are several of them in the social sciences. However, the anthropology of volume can use them as I suggested with action theories and, therefore, discover that a single volume accumulates them partially at a specific moment or for a few instants afterwards. This is what a detailed, and *a fortiori* uninterrupted, observation can identify. Among other analogous theorizations, I am thinking about the four schemas or types of relations (naturalist, analogical, totemic, or animist) of humans with non-humans, such as those identified by Philippe Descola [DES 05]. The anthropology of volume could indicate a few points: that a single human being from anywhere in the world can deploy these four schemas, one or another, at times nearly simultaneously, in some situations, over a single; that, even when these schemas have been added up, they do not represent the entire volume at this moment but only a specific volument; that they merely last, whether separately or together, a few moments in the daily continuity of a human volume; and also that they are not concretized as fully as their logics would allow and that they are lessened, distanced or unfinished (as we will see), compresent with other voluments in their concrete deployment. Adding this nuance is not an afterthought. In my opinion, it constitutes one of the most astonishing points that derive from working on the scale of the human volume, which involves taking into account first that humans themselves should be foregrounded before "non-humans" are introduced as a topic in anthropology. This implies associating "existants" with an existence that is entire, continuous and not characterized by a specific volument. It really seems to me that describing a detailed type of complexity, that is, the complexity of a human volume, raises time and again the question of the accuracy of descriptions, analyses and theories.

4.1. What the idea of volume tries to point out is the importance of not elaborating a description, explanation or theory based on a single volument or the interrelation of two or maybe three voluments, which requires at first a given perspective and therefore limits a volume, sometimes even as if these voluments constituted the whole human being: rationality, cognition, action, experience, subjectivity, the sensory-motor system, embodiment or the lived body in certain theories; embodied cognition according to other theories; and ethics, responsibility, freedom, the unconscious, habits or social trajectory in yet other theories. Therefore, some theoretical angles, to which we could easily assign authors and schools of thought, for example put aside feelings and regard them as non-existent in a volume that is limited to visible actions or linguistic acts. According to others, who emphasize action or responsibility, it is, for instance, social dispositions that may be forgotten. On the contrary, sometimes it is the actual accomplishment of actions that is hardly taken into account, if the focus is on the rationality of an actor or the reasons behind certain acts. Similarly, if we only consider social or cultural features, for example, those that are typical of social classes or cultures, we run the risk of losing the variety of voluments anchored in a volume, especially style, stylistic expressions as well as details that, in presences and according to the moment, could elude the pervading voluments. The empirical, as it were, and ever-continuing volume is more than body (or one of his specific parts) and cognition, body and subjectivity, or lived experience, whether these are added, combined or integrated. These types of focus, which often concern specific points and questions relevant to particular situations, may lose secondary gestures, the multiplicity of thoughts or perceptions, undoubtedly also the details of stylistic expressions and several other voluments that make up the density of volumes. We often need to consider entirety and continuity to find out the force of details, the density of voluments, but also the interplay of variable intensities and disintensities. The issue is not to eliminate several aspects that may elude some common types of emphasis, but precisely to insist on elements that may seem like details and the constantly modulated and attenuated compresences of these aspects within. This is exactly the goal of the four pairs of parameters and their associations, but it simultaneously allows us to point out that in a given moment, specific aspects and voluments may become more or less important than others.

4.2. From a methodological point of view, naturally, nothing precludes an exploratory observation based on a common type of ethnography and a basic understanding of what the volume in question says and does. However, this is not the main point when the goal is a detailed description of his acts and feelings. For a work of this kind, anthropologists, who can rely on their methodological and conceptual competences, are observers of a human volume who represents an external reality that is independent of them. The accuracy of the descriptions of anthropologists could be evaluated against the complex reality of the volume and his features. To carry out a double exploration of voluments, of what is visible but also invisible, of what a volume, one at a time, does and shows, of what he feels, which is not necessarily visible, the detailed observation of a volume, an emphasis on his acts and a description in the third person must also be completed by a decoding of the mental acts, moods, emotions and thoughts which are parts and voluments of a volume and cannot always be observed directly. Thus, in addition to an observation that should be as detailed as possible, film-like, and as uninterrupted as possible – something that is nearly indispensable a method based on explicitation interviews seems very relevant to me, but other types of interviews could also be suitable[13]. These may help identify states of mind that were implicit and help someone to verbalize thoughts or feelings that were forgotten or put aside, including those that perhaps have nothing do with situation.

> Even now, I am still greatly fascinated by the practice of the explicitation interview: questioning a person who begins with the affirmation that she does not know how she did what she did or what happened (subjectively non-conscious to her), and to gradually hear her describe her actions, with precision, as the interview unfolds, while discovering simultaneously (she and I) the detail of her lived experience. This is exactly what we are looking to do with the explicitation interview: the verbalization of the lived experience of action will occur during an awareness that is provoked by the elements of which the subject does not

---

13 We can refer to [PET 06] and [PET 15]. This is a critical study of the epistemological issues involved and of different types of discussion and introspection.

yet know that he knows them and even believes that he does not know them! [VER 18, p. 54]

In these discussions, which must be adapted if we wish to work with long-term prospects, researchers may, I believe, find different issues involved. However, I think it is important (if our aim is to describe with precision individual moments in their temporality and density of the instant) not to forget the objective, that is, that what is said should correspond as much as possible to what has actually been experienced. A person may also have to face films or pictures of his continuing presence. Therefore, based on a gesture or look, we can bring out some implicit elements but also the emotions related to an action, feelings of different intensities, the degree of clearness of an intention, in order to describe how a specific individual was at one time and then at another. The difficulty involved in describing with precision long durations does not mean that this is impossible. Naturally, the result is always imperfect and incomplete. This can also be confidently done by a researcher, of course, but without the empathetic dimension such as it is valued in an ethnographic relation [PET 06].

1.3. Difference and separation

1. Anthropological volumes have a significant characteristic: each volume differs from other volumes; there is this specific volume, that specific volume and so on. Importantly, they must be considered as such. In a situation that implies a so-called collective action, there are only individual and singular volumes, as each volume mixes several other voluments with gestures shared with the other volumes. Some of these voluments may have been present and integrated with their expressions into a volume for a long time. For example, this is the case for social characteristics or style. Other voluments are more variable, for instance, an emotion or a mood, and specific voluments can also be combined. I have pointed this out, but I will mention it again later. I think that the set of voluments does not unproblematically correspond to the difference between the "individual", "psychological" and "social" sphere, as Durkheim [DUR 08, p. 16] or Mauss [MAU 50, p. 329] claim in their works. This is a recurrent point in the lines of thinking of several sociologists and anthropologists, sometimes in debates with psychology or psychoanalysis. On the one hand, a volume represents an entirety, and this is what an individual is. This is the whole that constitutes an individual. It is not that some parts are individual and other parts are not.

They are all part of a volume. On the other hand, a volume includes several voluments, which originate and express themselves in different ways. These voluments cannot actually be reduced to a type of polarity, especially between what we may call psychological and social, even if these compresences reveal, as we will see, the pervading dimension of style, sociocultural traces, or roles, but they are themselves combined with one another and anchored in the volumic unity. In any case, we can only gauge the density of a volume with precision through the diversity of voluments and their variable compresences. As we have pointed out, it is this combination, with the detailed expressions of each volument, and especially with those voluments that remain the same, like stylistic traits, which allows us to describe a volume or his volumage, at the given time t and in the following moments. However, all this implies that we should consider at once the volume himself, a specific volume and not another, as the starting unity instead of a specific volument in particular, isolated from the entirety and continuity of the volume.

1.1. This perspective differs, for example, from that adopted by Ralph Linton, who belongs to the "culture and personality" school of thought of American anthropology. While putting forward a definition of personality – as he writes, "every personality presents two aspects, its content and its organization. The content consists of the personality's component elements; its organization, of the way in which these elements are related to each other and oriented both with respect to each other and to the total configuration" [LIN 36, p. 464–465] – Linton's argument involves relating personalities (e.g. the Madagascans or the Comanche) to their "common denominator" [LIN 36, p. 474], which constitutes a cultural affiliation and is nuanced according to the classes or groups an individual belongs to as well as various statuses or roles [LIN 45]. Thus, when some anthropologists elaborate a theory on the relations between individuals and a so-called society, when they resort to the classic notions of socialization or cultural integration and their synonyms and when they attempt to understand the different ways in which personalities are conditioned, they mostly attribute common characteristics which are cultural or related to a group. If the observers need to point out some differences in relation to these shared traits, these nonetheless remain the reference standard. In fact, this type of reading does not place the volumic unity at the center of the analysis. A focus on a specific volume will necessarily be different, as it does not prioritize shared traits or consider so-called individual variations as "secondary" in relation to these shared cultural traits, but it is immediately marked by the volumage as the specific compresence of voluments. For example, in a volume, a trait which may be regarded as typical of a culture or social class is not strictly speaking a replica, as it is always combined with other elements with which it contributes to this volumage. This same trait may at a given time manifest itself and disappear at another time. It is these nuances of voluments in a volume, together with the permeation, as we will see, of some of them, like style, which assign to this volume a type of singularity. Regarded as a unique volumic entity, the human being is not in any case interchangeable or exchangeable, unlike individuals considered in a role, activity, experience or as part of a culture in a classic anthropological description or analysis.

1.2. The term "volume" also helps us see that it is not enough to say that there are different individuals and set down their "irreducibility", but that we need to learn to look at them and consider their detailed voluments. Once again, this is the very question tackled by anthropology, which differs then from that of the social sciences: looking at and conceiving the volumic entity and not only its different modalities of "togethering" with other volumes. A volume cannot be reduced to collective issues, such as those concerning a situation or social or cultural affiliations, as is shown by the activated and blended multiplicity of voluments at each moment. I will come back to this point. However, what I mean to say is that this difference, that is, the "more or less" in relation to collective issues, can be found out. More globally, I would say that there is no unknowable irreducibility, ungraspable excess or "mystery", as we occasionally hear[14]. Of course, there is a seemingly infinite type of knowledge, which is not immediately complete. However, the anthropological volume does not contain a hidden part which becomes inaccessible for an observer[15]. As he faces each whole volume whom he observes in his acts and emotions, and together with his details, the anthropologist is aware of the difficulties involved in observing and describing these aspects. Unlike people who yield to indifference and accept not to understand and know, he should examine, look, observe, film, listen and question through his knowledge and competences, aiming for a type of knowledge that must always be supplemented by new observations and descriptions. Before giving any detailed description with the most accurate words possible and analyzing the various peculiarities of each volume, as I have just said, I do not see any other methodological means than a

---

14 For this estimate, the reader can, for example, refer to [RAP 15].
15 See Pierre Cassou-Noguès's words about looking at the sea, in a debate with *Object Oriented Ontology* [CAS 16, pp. 210–212].

painstaking observation which compares separate volumes together with their voluments.

2. A volume has another basic feature: he is a separate unit whose outline can be traced. It is through this type of delimitation that this unit can be grasped as volume. The Latin prefix *se-* means "without, apart, aside" (it recurs in *sepono*, "to put aside", or *seduce*, "to draw aside, to take aside" and consequently also "to seduce"). Naturally, the idea of "without" is not secondary. Separating (*se-pars*) means putting one part, in this case a human volume, aside and taking him apart, without the other parts, as a human being apart from any other human being [OXF 12]. When we see conjoined twins, whose birth derives from an accident during the embryonic process, the feeling of observing something curious, a "morphological variation" from the "internal cohesion" of life, reminds us that a common denominator of human beings and many living beings is their separation, according to Canguilhem's words [CAN 09, p. 134-135]. This is a condition of our existence that is shown by the irregularity of conjoined twins. One of Nabokov's novels was written based on the story of one of the Siamese twins, who tells their relation with these words: "a tendency to throw our heads back and avert our faces as much as possible was a natural reaction" and also "we never really spoke to each other, even when we were alone" [NAB 58]. Once detected, pregnancies that involve conjoined twins are in most cases terminated, as if it were "normal" for human beings to be units that are separate from one another.

2.1. A human volume is a separate entity with boundaries that separate him from other volumes. This separation, however, does not imply that there are no acts towards others or that others do not direct their actions at them. There is no question of conceiving a human being as closed and independent, not concerned by what happens outside him. It is separation itself that makes movement possible, as Nabokov's Siamese twins show. A volume is a separate unit but not a closed one. Yet, the empty space that separation necessarily creates between volumes prompts questions about the relevance of terms like "link", "connection", "interaction", or even more so "attachment", "penetration" or "fusion". These words seem to focus on this empty space as if it did not exist, were not empty or had been filled. Relations between separate volumes can only be attempts to reach one another. Let us recall Rilke's words about those people who "try to reach each other with words and gestures. They almost tear their arms out of their sockets, because the reach of their gesticulations is much too short. They never stop trying to throw syllables at each other, but they are extraordinarily bad at this game: they cannot catch" [RIL 09, part X]. Rilke comes back to this point: "Human beings are separated by such frightening distances [...] They give all they have and still cannot bridge it" [RIL 93c, p. 302]. Should we then refer to relations?[16] Once again, Latin may shed some light on the matter. *Relatum* is the past participle of two verbs. Only one of them gave rise to the term relation, but both are interesting. *Refero, retuli, relatum* means relating, recounting, but also bringing back, going back, bringing something back to where it first was – I think this is a very important point – whereas *relaxo, relavi, relatum* means to release, to free, to loosen, to be going at a slacker pace" [OXF 12]. This etymology allows us, on the one hand, to refute the relation of the vocabulary of connection as well as to draw the attention to movement as departure from and return to oneself and, on the other hand, to associate this movement with a form of distance. It seems to me that these lexical comments reveal an important fact: action or relation do not leave the volumic unity. This has nothing to do with pejorative labels such as egoism or individualism and applies equally to the most generous and "collective" individuals, or those who most overtly rely on gestures and are in movement. A volume is and remains a separate volume, as is shown by the movement of these actions, which come back almost naturally to him. It is as if messages, some "rays" sent from a volume and "directed" at another, without going as far as that, returned to their starting point. A link is not an actual link. A volume is an entity with a unitary structuration. He could not be any different from what he is, expressing himself as such in a sort of withdrawal or retreat into himself.

2.2. In concrete terms, what happens during an action which may be called, according to the authors, an interaction or a relation? While reasserting the primary importance of the volumic unity, I would like to point out the "retained" – in the original and nearly physical sense of the term – dimension that characterizes the way in which the unity is "held back" and "restrains itself". This is a significant point which I will refer to once again in section 1.4. A volume accomplishes actions with gestures and facial expressions – which are visible – and also with other voluments, thoughts or perceptions, which leave different traces. These voluments manifest themselves in and with the action in progress. Thus, we can see that

---

16 I have commented on and criticized elsewhere the relationism of some theories (Goffman, Lévi-Strauss, Bourdieu, Latour) and the limits they impose on a volume (see [PIE 14a, PIE 16, pp. 27–36]).

all the characteristics of these presences are not marked exclusively by the fulfillment of a role through the actions that it determines or the knowledge and know-hows that it implies. The perception of a situation, the knowledge of what a situation involves and the main expression of the role, with the adjustments that this entails, appear then to be the voluments of the volume himself. They seem like a part of this volume that is directly marked, retained and held by this role in progress[17]. However, there are other voluments as well. For example, this action in progress cannot be carried out without a stock of other actions or feelings that can be associated with the continuity of the volume himself, his previous instants or his other roles put on hold, which may or may not leave traces that are sometimes minimal in this moment of presence, and at times associated with various peripheral gestures, affects or different thoughts. With these supplementary details, it is as if this action about to be carried out were redirected by a volume who restrains himself from being exclusively present in a single action, in order to "turn back to himself", as it were. Among the other voluments in a volume, we can also often recognize the traces of social trajectories or cultural traces, which are well established in the volume. They may affect the roles and actions expected in a situation but also explain gestures, words and perceptions that do not correspond to these roles, thus pervading variable forms of distance and difference. There is also another volument, the style of a volume (his way of being present), which is also well established and can be dissociated from social and cultural marks. I will come back to this point later on. Undoubtedly, many gestures, words and thoughts, together with details of all kinds and ways of taking distance or even challenging, may not correspond to the roles involved in a situation – however, this does not imply going out of the volume – or be explained through social trajectories or cultural codes. Yet, they may correspond, when they emerge and when they are accomplished, to the style specific to a volume. I would also say that all these actions, which do not tally with an expected role, are retained, held, kept, marked or limited by a volume and, in this case, by the other pervading voluments, other than the role. Thus, this is also why minor gestural details of a volume, that is, the large number of non-relevant gestures that are associated with a style become the marks of personal singularity. Observing a volume implies retrieving a possible association of an action and its modes with a role that he expresses, parallel gestures, minor details and other voluments such as sociocultural marks and

---

17 Naturally, in a situation, the roles of different people are not necessarily the same, not to mention that they are linked to their other voluments.

style, but also states of mind. I will also refer back to these points. However, I would like to point out that at a given time t, a volume is the whole unity observed, who can do other things in addition to and alongside a specific action about to be carried out, that he constitutes more than actions or relations, as he is full of other voluments, and that he retains his actions and relations, regardless of their kind, as they are carried out, through other voluments of his, especially pervading voluments. Such is a human volume, separate from another: expressing, acting or rather trying and simultaneously singularizing an act, and therefore reintegrating it into his unity, resisting – even if this word is strong – links and relations.

2.3. A relation also appears as an attempt when a human volume, who is separate, is exposed to external elements, especially the effect of the voluments of other volumes whom he perceives and feels. He keeps some traces in the shape of an emotion, a new habit, perhaps a stylistic nuance, a thought, based on the gestures and words expressed by another volume, or events that have been perceived, seen and heard. However, he receives them and integrates them partially and laterally. He adjusts the intensity of what happens. I would like to recall Ralph Waldo Emerson's *Experience*, in which he writes that "the soul is not twinborn but the only begotten" [EME 83, p. 79] and that "all private sympathy is partial" [EME 83, p. 781]. Not merely separate and "solitary", a volume seems to have an eluding and distancing ability, as the Latin verb *relaxo* indicates. Thus, as Emerson writes, "our relations to each other are oblique and casual" [EME 83, p. 53] and "the dearest events are summer-rain, and we the Para coats that shed every drop". Focusing on a continuing volume clearly shows relation as merely an incomplete attempt, as this allows us to observe each volume as different and separate and to point out that what happens at every instant is swept along, left unfinished and lessened instant after instant.

2.4. A type of anthropology that emphasizes human unity should not describe what is "between", namely the interactional or relational process established from each participant's actions or words. It is as if this interactional and relation process replaced the empty space. Nor should it describe everyone's traits as pertinent to what may be called an "interaction" but it should concern the entire volume at the starting or end point or as he releases or absorbs what is sent or received. Thus, it is important (and difficult) to observe the traces or consequences of the gestures, words and acts of the volume in question or other volumes on himself and several voluments, thoughts, affects and moods, at a given time and in the following moments, on a short-, medium- or long-term basis. In addition to continuous films, in order to contribute to such a type of anthropology, we need the individuals whom researchers asked to take notes to take regular and detailed notes – writing "diaries". These notes, together with the anthropologists' observation, may involve choosing a word, gesture, activity or event, observing them as they unfold in a volume, and seeing their impact on or the absorption rhythm by the volume himself. They may be immediately forgotten or buried, but they may possibly resurface later on. They may also rapidly become something ruminated or meditated upon, set off an immediate act or gesture, or an immediate verbal response, create a cycle of interwoven thoughts or acts, leave their mark on the volume, or generate a new state, new rhythms or new habits. Something happens in a situation: this may be felt by a volume as a detail, it may be integrated as a point of reference and then forgotten, it may become something directly relevant, it may be perceived powerfully, it may be absorbed in a routinization process, but it may also be eliminated. Observing a human volume means observing voluments, as their importance varies time and again, and new traces as they take shape within him. These traces settle in the volume, with various distances and attenuations compared to the starting signs, which are occasionally repeated and to which a volume can be exposed several times. Therefore, it is also in this manner that the volumic unity, who is separate and not closed, is filled up with and emptied out of voluments. However, these observations seem to reveal that what is received and integrated at each moment is in most cases discreet, small and nearly negligible in comparison with the volumic unity and its own volumage. In other words, the volume always seems to prevail. Just as stylistic traits can pervade the changes that take place in a volume and absorb them in continuity, obliquity and laterality are significant ways of appropriating or re-appropriating – in the sense of making one's own – what happens. I will refer to these points in sections 1.4 and 1.5. The same goes for the formation and modification of the voluments of a volume. This distance is like a sign of the strength of the volumic unity. In other words, focusing on a volume forces us to look more closely. I am not interested in relation as something "between" or as something constitutive of humans (Latour's position), or in humans as they take part in interactions or relations (Goffman's position), but in the consistency of volumic entities, which resists what happens and relations [PIE 14a, PIE 16, pp. 28–37].

3. All this seems to reveal that what is "shared" in a situation – what a volume shares with others and what constitutes the primary focus adopted in

the social sciences – is then merely a part, exclusively a part, of the volume himself, which he activates thanks to expected voluments, perceptions (of the situation), gestures, attitudes, thoughts, values and sometimes feelings. This part is also an "imperfect" part, which is never really the same in different volumes, as it is mixed in each with other voluments that pervade it. Thus, this is the specific nature of what is "shared": running at a minimal level, because volumes are so intrinsically individual. Therefore, we can say either that this shared meaning works (it does not matter if it runs at a minimal level), thus focusing on what is shared, and the activated voluments, and nearly forgetting about the rest, or that it runs at a minimal level, thereby regarding this feature as essential. A direct focus on volumes and whole volumages, and not exclusively on what each shares with others, favors this option. In any case, an anthropologist who looks closely can identify what does not fall into a "togethering" with others in a situation – that is, the voluments that are not part of what has been shared in an interaction. In each situation, this seems to be the most important part. It is the very consistency of a volume, besides these shared elements, which will soon turn into another type of "shared elements" in the following situation.

1.4. Volumuation and continuity

1. I have mentioned on more than one occasion the consistency, continuity or style of a volume. Now, I need to consider these aspects in detail. As a separate and individual type of unity, a volume is not a mere series of moments of presence. He is precisely a volume with his continuity. How can this continuity be conceived according to the meaning given in the dictionary, that is, not only as uninterrupted duration but also as stability with possible changes in a unity that holds everything together, according to the etymological association of the Latin verbs *continuare* (to ensure continuity) and *continere* (to hold together, bound) [OXF 10, OXF 12]? This point will also allow us to show the specific features of a volumage. If we think about it, a human volume is at first a new cell, which is immediately unique thanks to its genome and range of possibilities, born from the meeting of sperm and oocyte. The chances of finding two identical genomes deriving from this fertilization are of 1 in 70 billion… based on the same two parents [CAM 05, p. 248]. Before dividing, this cell has a lifespan ranging from 12 to 24 hours. Already, there is an individual, an "informed" volume, indissociable matter and form, one unable to exist without the other, to use Aristotle's words

[ARI 00][18]. Physically cohering and therefore pervaded by the initial genetic identity, the divided cells will then remain part of this unique volume, whose outline can be traced. Yet, it is important not to neglect some current perspectives used in biology and their results, which are sometimes used to emphasize non-uniqueness and non-continuity: each human body contains a significant share of bacteria; the genome of human cells contains elements of viral origin; it can itself be expressed in different ways depending on the cells and also change partially at each moment of its existence according to an individual's own experiences – including in its fetal stage – or in a radically unpredictable manner and with more or less significant consequences. Therefore, two "actual" twins, born from the same fertilization process and with the same initial genome, will already be slightly different at birth. Employing such information in anthropology to consider human beings as heterogeneous changing forms, presented as "masses of living forms" and even "microbes" has always surprised me [PAL 13a, PAL 13b]. On the one hand, this way of considering a human and microbes as equivalent, as G. Palsson[19] suggests, seems to be one of those simplified and risky shifts in scale that biologists themselves question. It is the same mistake, with another shift in scale, involved in thinking that the human dimension and the social or cultural sphere are equivalent. However, once again, based on rigorously established cross-disciplinary protocols and with the aim of avoiding arguments that may seem literally dubious, why not observe the continuity of a human volume and simultaneously the continuity of his microbes or that of his brain plasticity? In any case, anthropologists would only consider his scale. This seems to play a significant role in the argument that I am trying to develop in this book. On the other hand, the presence of bacteria, the continual renewal of human cells (which is only fragmentary at a given time and cannot destabilize the cohesion and organization of the body) and especially the genetic changes in each individual (once again partial) do not compromise the unity, coherence and continuity of the anthropological volume. Beyond and with the variations of a volume, it is the unity and consistency that an anthropologist should face from the first moments in which a volume can be observed.

---

18 In [PIE 17], I attempted to show the relevance of some points of Aristotle's *Metaphysics* for anthropology.

19 "If humans are assemblies or aggregates of life forms, the outcomes of ensembles of biosocial relations, then they have not simply co-evolved with more-than-human microbes; human are microbes" [PAL 13b, p. 241].

2. Therefore, continuity defines simultaneously this uninterrupted series of his acts and forms of presence but also a given stability of and within the volume. Looking at this volume from his birth and day after day should be the work of anthropologists *par excellence*. As I have often pointed out, ideally, we would obtain a film of each human showing all his life uninterruptedly. This may be impossible. Yet, what is most astonishing is that this currently is not a goal for anthropologists, who find this perspective objectifying or perhaps even irrelevant. On the contrary, I find this to be crucial. Thus, the anthropology of volumes will favor uninterrupted films of an individual's existence or at least long and continuous periods of time in his existence. Such observation methods seem incompatible with some specific fields of study, for example, psychoanalysis, which not only analyzes mostly the psychological life and its afflictions but does so in particular moments. As Patrick Declerck notes: "it is impossible to follow a case or a patient over time. It would take too long, it would be too complicated, and too long-term" [DEC 01, p. 77]. I think this is one more reason why we should do this in anthropology. This direct and detailed focus on the volume himself is naturally based on a different scale than cells, but it also differs from what is sometimes defined as "relational becoming" in an environment, with the ensuing possibility that this process (and also changes or differences) become the primary focus without "grasping" the reality of the volume himself, his consistency and his continuity. Observing a volume on a microcontinuous level is undoubtedly a powerful way of finding out and understanding the share of voluments in his constitution, in particular their changes and their non-changes. From his first instant and during all his existence, a volume of being, who is always there, shows what I call "volumuations", based on the apt word suggested by Catherine Beaugrand. These are microvariations of a volume or of voluments situation after situation[20]. It is this detailed observation of temporal continuity that reveals the other continuity, namely that of the volume with voluments that remain the same beyond possible changes. Between volumuation and the continuity of the volume there are several points which can be identified. The fundamental issue is to take this empirical continuity of the anthropological volume seriously: what will we discover then?

---

20 I prefer leaving the French word *volumuation* (which is a portmanteau combining "volume" and "to molt" – *muer* in French) untranslated in order to highlight the significant notion of molting, as it refers to superficial or partial changes.

2.1. First, the volumuations of some elements of the volume observed do not preclude the continuity of other parts. In other words, these other parts do not change. For example, a human being does this and then does that, moving from a concentrated attitude to an absent-minded mood, accepting what happens and then deciding to change, feeling one emotion and then another and so on. These examples of changes do not concern the whole volume. Some other aspects or voluments of this volume are not involved in these changes which, besides, can be reversible. The volumage at the surface of the volume, for example, on the face, with some traits that are changeable and others that are less so, seems to restore its balance uninterruptedly in a state that hardly changes. What we observe moment after moment are naturally volumuations, namely "molts" that are not total and do not concern the whole volume. Thus, after each volumuation, some parts of the volume remain the same. An observer may see which of them change, which return to their previous state and which do not, or which do not change and seem to remain the same, instant after instant. In this sense, undoubtedly, Rodin's sculptures show in a powerful manner that the movements of a volume do not go out of what seems to be his unity. More precisely and in relation to change, Gsell describes in dialogue with Rodin in *The Age of Bronze*:

> The legs of this adolescent who is not completely awake are still soft and almost vacillating. But as the glance moves upward, one sees the attitude grow stronger: the ribs lift under the skin, the thorax dilates, the face is directed toward the sky, and the two arms stretch to shake off their torpor. [ROD 84, p. 30]

Rodin points out: "he [the painter or sculptor] makes visible the passage of one pose into the other; he indicates how imperceptibly the first glides into the second. In his work, one still detects a part of what was while one discovers in part what will be" [ROD 84, p. 29]. Also: "Movement is the transition from one attitude to another. This simple statement, which sounds like a truism, is indeed the key to the mystery" [ROD 84, p. 28]. Movement after movement, it is as if there were a link or a transition that leaves a trace of the presence of the previous action while anticipating the following. Associated with a role or an activity, the movements in question may be pervaded by the details of previous or following presences, for example gestures but also thoughts, or the states of mind of other moments which may be more or less distant, as if to guarantee a common thread and some continuity. The same goes for stylistic traits, which may continue instant after instant, and also for roles or social traces. Besides, in most cases we need several instants, days and years for accumulated variations to become significant and perceptible. Naturally, from new-borns to aged people, including adolescents and adults, the rhythm and effects of some volumuations, as well as their intensities, differ. Observing these volumuations would ideally imply identifying what changes and what remains the same from one situation to another, regarding gestural movements, facial expressions, and also moods and thoughts. Naturally, the proportion of what remains identical and what changes will vary if we consider two moments that follow each other and two moments separated by 10 or 15 years. This leads me to the following point.

2.2. The human volume, who is not a multiplicity juxtaposing voluments, is marked by the presence and continuity of certain voluments that pervade some other voluments. This is their specific characteristic. Thus, the multiplicity and diversity of voluments seem nearly connected and contained by the pervading voluments. I find this point significant and empirically verifiable. It is in this context in particular that style, which has already been mentioned previously, plays a part with its pervading force and ability to mark other voluments, including the volumuations that take place. Here, I do not regard style as a perception issue but in its objective reality[21]. With its various, singular manifestations, which are specific to each particular volume, stylistic continuity includes gestural, linguistic or cognitive modes, bodily expressions and psychological traits, habits, and ways of feeling and being moved well established in a volume and more or less – but never completely – stabilized as existence unfolds. Should I also include as part of a volume's style memories, reasons why I carry out a specific action, and desires or types of knowledge in particular that characterize a volume, as all this can permeate actions with a certain repetition and ensures continuity in

---

21 In a recent issue of *Social Anthropology* (yet unpublished as I write this) on "character", this word is mostly understood as a notion used by individuals, favored in some cultures more than others, called on in local situations, and assigned and ascribed in acts of mutual acknowledgment, as if the issue for constructivist and situationist approaches were to avoid an essentialist reading that emphasizes "consistency" (see [REE 18]). On the contrary, I want to focus on the objectivity of stylistic expressions that can be described, if I look closely at a human being without interruptions, and play a significant part in my understanding of how volumes go on. I draw attention to the paper of Huon Wardle [WAR 18] about the importance of the "individual character" in the Caribbean everyday, considered beyond the "anthropological terms such as 'intersubjectivity' or 'relational personhood'", and all of this being in debate with the readings of some anthropologists who emphasize the "cultural character" and the "social personhood".

this volume? I think so. In any case, some stylistic expressions may be identical or nearly the same for several decades, whereas memory, ideas or desires, while they keep a set of old traces and specific ways of unfolding, are more changeable as they are also in a direct continuity with what has come before. Discussing the origin of these stylistic expressions could be useless without uninterrupted filmic data. In any case, I will distinguish between stylistic expressions (whose origin and formation derive, for example, from what we call "temperament" or "character", from gestural or bodily movements that take place over the course of time, and then stabilizes progressively, or from the accumulation of specific experiences, as all of them can be intertwined) and the other traits, capacities or dispositions themselves which are inherited from what is called social classes or cultural codes. These sociocultural aspects can also be found in other volumes, even if, as we know, they are not exactly identical in each volume. What is involved in this case is a specific type of actions, tastes, values, decisions or habits in the various situations of daily life. Distinguishing between style and social and cultural marks represents a point of view that differs from that adopted by Bourdieu, who regards personal style as the result of a series of social dispositions to which an individual has been exposed [BOU 77, pp. 284–285]. Furthermore, stylistic traits can infiltrate social marks, which would be different or heterogeneous in a volume and therefore would become "bound" in some sort. In any case, it is not always easy to distinguish between these traits, as they blend in with one another as well as with other voluments[22]. Continuous observation over long periods of time is a significant advantage in this sense. Focusing on a volume in this manner does not exclude taking into account lived experience and the perception of continuity, through an often implicit feeling of one's existence and memories, but it emphasizes the continuing presence of stylistic modes that concern one's position, gestures, words and various feelings, including the

---

22 In *Ethical Life*, Webb Keane, relying on Goffman, emphasizes interactional process and especially the work of "faces" which emerge, protect one another, and therefore, construct one another. This creates "the public exo-skeleton of character" (see [KEA 16, p. 97]). If this reading may help us understand some ways in which a volume may be stable, it runs the risk of not taking into account the details related to the different stylistic expressions that constitute presences as well as the strength with which these expressions remain the same in situations. Style cannot be reduced to actions or interactions that take place and recur and to what is interactionally relevant. It is actually the details and the continuity of their expression that are especially at stake when I observe style. Furthermore, before and besides their modes, roles themselves often emerge also in the continuity of stylistic traits that are specific to a volume (e.g. cognitive or psychological traits). In any case, uninterrupted observations are key if we want to consider all these aspects.

perception of continuity but also discontinuity[23]. Someone has just got married. He has a career change. He naturally remains tall or short, smart or thick, but especially he still retains his way of being tall or short, smart or thick, which is his and does not seem to reveal the presence of a strictly social mark. Several characteristics – the way of smiling, making a gesture, or holding a spoon – remain in the details of acts which themselves recur in the situation and may also establish their own habits and routines. Gerald Manley Hopkins, an English poet who wrote in the 19th Century, describes a way of speaking as follows:

> I was noticing his pronunciation when he reads aloud. In words like *Ribadeneira* he gives to the *ei* the value of both letters, making the true diphtong between *a* and *i*. He flattens the final consonants, as led for let. The soft g, as in *raging*, is very noticeable: it is a Greek dzêta I think, almost = *dz*. [HOP 59, p. 159]

This is a stylistic expression, as long as in this case it is not associated with a cultural and social sign or with a regional accent, etc. Besides such particular expressions, style can also be recognized when it percolates through several voluments, although not all, constituting a way of being present in one's actions, without, however, representing a totality that pervades everything, as Sartre claimed. A volume carries out a specific activity, he goes somewhere, feels a certain emotion, but he is still this way or that way. His activity, his movement and his emotion are pervaded by a specific stylistic trait, bodily traits, or a given trait of his character, which can be recognized with their details in actions, feelings or postures, which, as they are already present in a volume, could be identified in other circumstances and also in other successive moments. Thus, in its modality but also in its origin, an act, which includes several voluments, may be directly associated with an individual's character or temperament, defining ways of being that recur in various situations and can pervade and link some voluments: being optimistic or pessimistic, calm or agitated, and especially a way of being optimistic or pessimistic, and calm or agitated. Therefore, sad or happy thoughts, which are typical of a certain temperament, together with their manners of being sad or happy, may mark other voluments. This percolating modality may also correspond to a set of ideas and values shaped over time, which may then arise again in various acts, actions or words.

---

23 See [FUC 16] for synoptic debate about the philosophical and psychiatric issues involved.

Therefore, a style, which corresponds to a range of specific traits that straddle roles and acts, seems to hold a volume together, naturally never in a totally fixed manner, as his modifications remain at his surface and fragmentary at every moment. While keeping a volume together, the stylistic traits themselves can impact a situation and not necessarily the same traits depending on the moments. Could we imagine a human volume without stylistic traits? This interconnection of pervading voluments also manifestly takes place when there are mental and psychiatric problems, according to the names we prefer to use, which could be characterized at first glance by "dislocation". It is as if the stylistic traits asserted or recalled every time that the various voluments as well as their actions and words belong to the volume and are his. I could interpret this as a form of positive resistance, of course implicit, to events. Naturally, I could say that in a human volume, nothing, including genes, belongs to him, but also that everything belongs to the volume himself, as he can only appropriate and re-appropriate. This is the way a volume functions in unity.

2.2.1. I will point out three things. First, the continuity of a volume does not prevent an individual from feeling here and there a certain discontinuity, not perceiving his unity, not "recognizing" himself, as is sometimes the case, for example, in situations that involve psychological problems. However, second, as I have claimed, a volume's way of not recognizing himself, which involves a volument among other voluments, is characteristic of him and part of his continuity. This does not imply that a feeling of continuity and identity, which may be more or less implicit, diffuse but occasionally more explicit, does not help the volume become somewhat more "solid". Ultimately, this continuity is not a total type of continuity that does not vary throughout the volume. It is also related to the voluments in question.

2.2.2. Let us spell out this last point. Rilke writes about the presence of a style "everything in Nature grows and defends itself in its own way and is characteristically and spontaneously itself, seeks at all costs to be so and against all opposition" [RIL 62, p. 53]. Is this not excessive? Of course, style structures the diversity of the voluments and makes it possible to identify some continuity. However, it is not the only element that structures or ensures continuity, as there are also social or cultural marks, roles, types of knowledge and know-hows. Style itself or temperament can express themselves in several bodily, cognitive or psychological ways. Moreover, as I have just mentioned, style does not permeate a volume completely. It characterizes, pervades and singles out some voluments rather than others at a given time, as if it were making way for other pervading voluments. It is always important, even when a stylistic mark is quite defined, to look for something more or less, maybe something minuscule, that prevents or in any case nuances any exclusive interpretation[24]. Like social or cultural marks, style lets some of its specific traits or expressions, for example, bodily or cognitive in this or that situation, take shape or combine in particular associations with a gesture, word or thought. It can express itself in a specific gesture at a specific time with one trait rather than another, while other voluments combine with it. Therefore, it may appear with microdifferences, for example, depending on whether a gesture characterized by a specific stylistic trait is associated with another specific volument or action and accompanied by a specific emotion. A continuous observation, based on the stylistic expressions identified, considers which temperamental aspects, gestural modes or cognitive modes continue in a specific series of situations or reappear very often. Style does not represent all of a volume. It is mixed with other things, so that it can lose some of its strength and reduce its traits. It is exactly the power of the notion of volume that allows us to draw the attention to the dynamic between different voluments. Besides, I will say it again, the significance of style together with its different expressions does not turn style into a radically immutable volument, strictly speaking. A stylistic trait can always be nuanced or modified, in any case gradually. Do I need to point out that some traits percolating through several actions and other voluments are all the more stabilized as they took shape at the beginning of the volume's existence? Therefore, observing newborns is very important in this respect. I can then ask myself some questions.

When does a style, together with its bodily, gestural or cognitive expressions, become identifiable and recognizable? When does it stop changing in a significant manner? Later on, when an individual has grown up, which nuances or changes are possible? In the style of a continuing volume, which postural, cognitive or psychological traits are the most resistant? Which are the least resistant and likely to change or even disappear? We can also ask these questions about the social marks to which

24 These empirical remarks reduce any type of theory that associates the unity and entirety of the human being to a fundamental characteristic, for example "care" or "anxiety", as Heidegger discusses [HEI 10, p. 178 and ff.]. Based on what I have just said, either of these could evidently concern the style of one volume but not of another, more at a specific time instead of another. Similarly, they could not contain all the voluments of a volume, they would be present alongside other stylistic traits, and they would be themselves marked by details that characterize and single out someone's way of being worried or anxious.

new-borns are especially exposed and whose traces they accumulate. Besides, how do stylistic traits pervade those, which may be more or less compatible, of social trajectories and vice versa? At the other end, when there are diseases, which occasionally change our bodies, thoughts, or memory very suddenly, does a volume not reveal types of gestures or a body language that continue until the last moment?

Direct and uninterrupted observations, as well as comparisons between filmed clips, based on family videos, could give some answers to the questions asked with the required meticulousness. The remarks made in this section aim to encourage observations that are as exhaustive as possible or "stylographies" of a volume.

2.3. Gestures, words or actions may also have, after a given time t, consequences for a volume and his volumuations. I have already outlined this point. The actions, thoughts and emotions of a volume, or those of another volume, and the occurrence of some events have various, temporary, long-lasting, sudden or gradual effects on the continuity of the volume in question. However, as if this volume could suddenly detach himself from what happens to him, these consequences are partial and can have a short- or medium-term effect on a specific volument of the volume, entailing variable and sometimes negligible consequences, while leaving other characteristics intact. Over time and in different situations, numerous variations and movements of a volume have no consequences and may be reversed. Before being carried out, several actions are not that "essential" for a volume, instant after instant. Afterwards, naturally, nothing would have really been similar if certain specific actions had not been what they were, but the amount of change between before and after is often minimal. Aristotle uses this example: "someone is digging a trench for a plant and finds treasure. This finding of the treasure is an accident for the man who digs the trench. It is not the case that finding treasure necessarily comes from or after digging a trench, nor would one for the most part in doing some planting find treasure" [ARI 04, 1025a]. Because of this coincidence or extravolumic accident, this individual has become rich, started carrying out new actions, and taken on new roles. However, he has also maintained some of the old ones, together with his way of carrying them out. What a volume integrates over the course of time and situation after situation, even in an unexpected way, may re-orientate some of his recent or older characteristics, but it is also marked and pervaded by other elements, especially his style in several of its expressions. Therefore, a volume acts, speaks and feels. He "volumuates", accumulating volumuations – which are always partial – over time and adaptation after adaption, but some stylistic traits remain the same or become slowly nuanced. The person who discovered the treasure has his specific, bodily and psychological way of finding it, seizing it and being happy. He even has his own way of changing some activities in his existence once he has become rich. Thus, style is a way of appropriating what happens and making it one's own, retaining and holding back the acts of the volume. This is also true for other pervading voluments, such as sociocultural marks and several types of knowledge and competence that are anchored in a volume. All of this makes up the continuity and variations of a volume. And I will keep looking at the volume and asking questions.

Which consequences or series of consequences does this discovery or other events entail? Which voluments will be concerned temporarily or lastingly? Which voluments will not be concerned? How do lived experience and feelings have an effect on other voluments? When a technical gesture, a way of speaking, or a line of thinking adapt to a situation and can consequently change, which part of style keeps pervading them? Can a stylistic trait (or a trait of a social habit) be modified little by little? How and to which degree of nuance or gradual change is it absorbed by other traits? At a given time t, with his own unity, style, stylistic expressions but also some voluments of his (his moods, emotions, know-hows, etc.), how does a volume integrate events that come from outside? How is the specific intensity of a moment appropriated in the consistency itself of a volume? Then, or in any other type of change, what is the role played by the different pervading voluments, as well as obliqueness, which I have mentioned above, or lessereity, which I will soon introduce?

3. To point out the dynamic that governs voluments, volumuations and the continuity of a volume, I will refer back to what the details of a presence reveal at a given time t. As we know, a volume is filled, among other voluments, by stylistic traits (with their aforementioned various expressions) but by also cultural and social traces as well as by the role of the situation, together with his types of knowledge, his characteristic know-hows, certain rules and the actions that he may carry out. Let us consider these as typically pervading voluments. They may combine, complete one another, arrange one another in hierarchies, nuance one another and perhaps contradict one another with their various expressions, while also pervading other voluments, gestures, affects, feelings, body posture, desires, wishes, etc., which are always more or less activated. Together, they may then pervade

and connect some of the volume's voluments. This is the general configuration. Other arrangements are possible. These allow us to observe a variety of compresences with pervading voluments, which may or may not be present, but they also show us that the actions of a volume remain marked in different ways by them and to some extent retained in the volume. Here are some examples.

– There are presences that involve several voluments, which seem very marked by the role and gestures that must be executed as well as the know-how involved in this role. These may also be lived as a duty. However, the activity itself also includes tiny traces of stylistic expressions. The same goes for presences that are socioculturally or stylistically very marked and that leave traces of other pervading voluments, which are less important. Naturally, there may be specific voluments that are exclusively pervaded by the role of the situation, or style, or by social or cultural marks. However, a presence in most cases includes compresences of different pervading voluments. In another situation, the same volume is characterized by a different arrangement where voluments are compresent and pervading to a different extent.

– Certain voluments, actions, words, gestures, feelings or thoughts may be dissociated from the role of the situation in question or be critical and in a tense relation with it. They may elude (or not) social or cultural habits, but, at their origin and in their accomplishment, they may correspond to a specific reason for acting, a specific character trait, or other stylistic expressions that can pervade several voluments, as we have seen above. This dissociation may concern some voluments but not necessarily all of them, for example, one gesture rather than another, one specific word instead of another, this emotion but not that idea.

– Besides actions and thoughts that play a central role in a situation and are marked by a role, sociocultural habits, or stylistic traits, or by one or two or all three of these types of voluments, a volume may simultaneously reveal other peripheral gestures and so-called secondary thoughts, which elude these three dimensions. Nonetheless, fleeting thoughts may refer to moments that have just happened or will happen, while gestures and a set of minor details, like these thoughts, may also indicate some stylistic traits.

– In another example, in new situations – even if this is not necessarily the case – I can observe actions that are unusual, without know-how, but distinctly marked by some of the volume's stylistic expressions as well as the opposite, namely a role with gestures, thoughts and words that do not seem significantly pervaded by stylistic traits or sociocultural traces. It may also happen that a specific role implies actions that are in conflict with some of the volume's stylistic tendencies. In these compresences of voluments, a role may dampen at a given time a stylistic trait that works against its fulfillment. However, in this case as well as in many others, a given role or a specific action, for example, this "dampening", is fulfilled with an explicit desire or wish and counts on well-established reasons for being present at this moment in this situation. It thus cannot be dissociated from the knowledge accumulated, certain ideas of the volume, other stylistic traits and also from his temporal continuity, which have all given rise to this role. If, for example, this allows this role to be experienced critically at another time, this feeling is perhaps also characteristic of the style of the volume in question.

– I can also point out that a volume will never make the "same" gesture in the same way. This may be due to the fact that it is combined with other voluments, thus producing nuances, but also because of the mere contingency involved in the movements, which introduce very small differences. For example, no gesture or specific movement that involves my fingers, arm or a way of sitting will ever be identical to another, even if they seem the same or appear to belong to a markedly typical aspect of a specific volume. Therefore, about this aspect, I can always observe minimal variations: the position of my fingers, a slightly different way of tilting my head or torso, or how tense my arm is[25]. It is these details and bits and pieces of actions or gestures that try to elude the volume's stylistic expressions rather than the volume himself. Perhaps, these variations in turn will recur and become fixed in a certain way.

– I think it is possible that no volument eludes the various pervading voluments. Are there any presences that elude all of this, the role and the know-hows adjusted to the situation, social permeation, cultural marks and the volume's own style? I think that there cannot be such a concurrence of possibilities. In particular, I do not think it is possible to avoid all stylistic expressions, and especially for all the voluments activated at a specific

---

25 For a detailed analysis of this example, see [PIE 17, p. 216 and ff.].

moment of presence. In reality, as it is connected to the unity of a volume and his continuity, a presence – including the cases in which the volume seems very active or creative – cannot be separated, as we have seen, from either a volume's types of knowledge, thoughts and memories, or the series of instants of the volume and, therefore, of other voluments which are present or come before the instant in question, specifically a state of mind, perception, emotion or traces of older events, reasons behind a specific action, and thoughts about future instants, as all of this becomes involved in a volume's style. I can also add to this the more or less diffuse perception of this continuity, which is undoubtedly marked itself by character and temperament.

Concretely, therefore, an immense empirical field opens up. Once again, this implies that we should consider all the voluments that contribute to a moment of presence to identify with precision that voluments are marked at a specific moment by the role, by the "sociocultural" dimension, by style, by one or two of these three and more specifically by a particular trait of the social trajectory, cultural codes or style. Through this lens, a moment of presence, in its density, could be, for example, a word, accompanied by the know-how of the role adapted to the situation, an unexpected posture – which, however, corresponds to well-established social traces – secondary gestures that typically characterize a volume, the strong feeling of a constraint, or of this social trajectory, or another emotion, which may be associated with the mood of the moment and a characteristic temperament, but also some fleeting thoughts that remain unexpressed. Shortly afterwards, the presence of a volume may involve fulfilling the same role and expressing stylistic traits, which complicate it or even contradict it, as the awareness of this discrepancy may result in a certain irony or tense criticism. The possible intensity of this awareness and perceptions seems to correspond to a volume's style and temperament. This presence may also involve a supplementary action that is culturally very marked and associated with specific cultural representations – with or without a reflexive consciousness – and another action in the very next moment, which is completely unaffected by this permeation of cultural codes but stylistically marked. This does not imply that the traces of style are not to some extent present in the action that took place in the previous moment. Such traces of continuity can still be seen in the various following permeations, with the variety of voluments and their different visible and perceived intensities. Let us point out that the same volume can also reveal the same volument, for example, body posture, which is here permeated more deeply by the role and there by style, in another situation again by social traces and afterwards by cultural codes. Besides, specific interdependencies between a specific pervading volument and a specific action, gesture or emotion can also be identified in a volume in particular. The previous or following moments, with the states of mind they create, also affect these mixtures. Another volume, at the same moment and in the same situation, will show a different compresence of voluments: a word and a gesture that have not been adjusted to the situation, together with a highly characteristic cultural mark and stylistic trait, a critical perception of either of them, a different mood associated with another previous moment, etc. Here are several details and avenues for observation as well as a deconstruction that aims to find unity again. I think this is essential if the aim is to understand this volumic unity. In fact, there is indeed unity, in which the pervading voluments take part. I want to use these examples to reveal the various ways in which a volume can mark his acts and continuity through volumuations. Moment after moment, in a volume, as these series suggest, there are few voluments whose emergence and realization are not marked and therefore retained by a specific pervading volument, which characterizes it, or by the traces of previous instants[26]. It is as if these voluments could not avoid being present in one way or another. Above, I have pointed out that style, together with its singular way of marking, is a volume's specific mode of appropriation. I could say that all these pervading voluments hold the volumic unity together. They represent in their own way some types of appropriation. The other voluments are thus somehow attached and linked to the volume. From one moment to the next, there are continuities and the continuous presences of these pervading voluments, stylistic expressions, roles or social and cultural traces. In particular, body posture, types of gestures, facial expressions, character traits and linguistic accent are singular stylistic marks that are often present and identifiable in a volume at a given time t and in the following moments, even if roles change according to the situations. In addition to the voluments concerned by the act of the moment and beyond as well as besides the variety of these compresences, there is always one volume who appears in his entirety with his consistency, knowledge, a memory, stabilized know-hows and habits, as well as some stylistic traits, even if the latter do not necessarily take shape at a given time t concurrently and throughout the volume and his voluments. In any case, a consistency, together with the expression of its continuity, can always be identified.

---

26 Unfortunately, there is a lack of accurate observations that could clarify all these points on a volume scale, uninterruptedly and naturally in real situations and not in a controlled setting.

3.1. In other words, I think it is important to emphasize simultaneously the variety of these compresences accompanied by pervading voluments and the fact that a volume's actions remain clearly contained and retained within him as volumuations occur. On the one hand, concentrating on the variable compresence or variable importance of these pervading voluments may undoubtedly have critical potential compared with theories that attach importance exclusively to the social or cultural spheres as well as roles or subjectivities. Uninterruptedly considering a volume and the dynamic of his voluments eschews precisely the establishment of a decisive type of exclusivity, whether due to a role, activity, social trajectory, cultural codes or stylistic traits (these may also include character or temperament, ideas, but also cognitive modes, and bodily expression, as I have shown). In fact, it is possible to observe that each pervading volument has different proportions and degrees of significance, one of which could become predominant for specific voluments but not for others, or for a group of them, in a specific situation but not in another. At a given time, a specific volument (e.g. an emotion or a thought), which would seem dissociated from some pervading voluments but not from the previous instants and the volume's ideas or memories, may even take on an important function for this volume, whereas other voluments pervaded by the role, the sociocultural dimension and other stylistic elements are present but less important. Thus, without any preconceptions about the necessity and hierarchy of specific voluments, an anthropology of the volume observes some indeterminacy of voluments pervading a volumuation at a given time. However, this indeterminacy is not merely a lack of voluments, especially the role, or style, or the sociocultural dimension, or an absence of continuity of the voluments' traces as they remain in a volume according to different degrees of significance. Besides, if I observe a volume carefully, I can see that adapting to the same role may happen randomly, in seemingly contingent ways, and with actions, or in any case words, gestures, thoughts or types of knowledge that vary. These presences may also be associated with the states of mind of the previous moments, without being dissociated from style itself. They may also adapt to the circumstances or microcircumstances of a situation, for example, with supplementary gestures. Yet, all of this does not imply going out of the role itself, or even style or social marks, and their pervading effect on these gestures. Similarly, the same stylistic tendency (or a social trajectory) may concretize itself in a volume with different traits according to a specific moment, the previous instants, states of mind, but also the role in question. These traits of the pervading voluments are also associated or combined with one another and other voluments that are expressed or activated at a specific time and may then seem slightly different according to these compresences. Therefore, in the same volume, where some voluments are continuous and others are well established, no presence is ever actually the same as another, not even in a similar situation. According to the situations, the same action or gesture is not compresent with the same perceptions and thoughts, as they are associated with potentially different states of mind, which depend, for example, on the previous or following moments. Once again, the previous instants may account for these differences, which indeed include some of the volume's stylistic expressions and become consequently less noticeable. This is, I believe, the contribution of a meticulous and detailed observation centered on the same volume compared in the various situations he finds himself in, in order to see and compare the ways in which voluments with their contingencies take shape. Therefore, if the focus is on a volume and his voluments, there is no strict programming or total predictability.

3.2. On the other hand, as I have pointed out, indeterminacy, with the acts that it involves, remains precisely pervaded, contained, restrained and determined, as it were, in and by a volume's stylistic expressions, his sociocultural characteristics and/or the roles fulfilled, the traces of their continuity, but also those left by moments that have just or long gone by. A volume cannot avoid himself, the voluments he contains, which mark him as well, his singularity or the traces of previous instants. If I observe volumuations and the series of moments following one another, it seems excessive to support the notion of freedom or associate it with indeterminacy. I actually think that the opposite is true when I observe a human volume in his continuity and with his acts, about to be marked and pervaded by specific voluments of his, depending on them and the previous instants. What may resemble or be perceived as freedom is then only a mode among many, anchored in a volume and dependent on him and especially his style. The same applies to what may be called choice or decision but also to any specific permeation: these cannot be separated from the entirety of a volume in connection with his other voluments, the habits he has acquired over his long life, his style, his states of mind before an action and some traces of previous events.

3.3. Therefore, an anthropological volume has a continuing consistency – a volumic consistency – which includes stabilized voluments that pervade his volumuations and connect them within him. These volumuations are appropriated and consequently somehow retained, regardless of what they are, at their origin and during their concretization. There is also a continuing existence instant after instant through interrelated series of voluments – actions, thoughts, memories, states of mind, moods – bouncing between, as I have pointed out, present, past or future situations, accompanied by awareness and perceptions of different forms of this continuity, which may be more or less diffuse or clear-cut. Undoubtedly, this awareness or feeling as well as these successions of presences will take shape at least through one of the volume's stylistic modes. This idea of consistency and continuity does not imply that I should first mention a tension between an individual and a society, or a definition – or the fact of being "determined" by or transcending over, as Nigel Rapport[27] would say, what may be called "society". What I observe and attempt to describe and conceptualize is above all a life contained and a volume determined by himself and his voluments. Opposing the idea of totality, Tim Ingold thinks that life is always eluding us: "For it posits a complete human whose very existence is encompassed and contained" [ING 18, p. 120]. His point of view is undoubtedly easier to accept than the intra-determined and intra-limited volume I describe. This volume is caught in several and differentiated intra-determinations and intra-limitations, for example, those concerning sociocultural marks, stylistic expressions or roles, with their contingencies which, however, are precisely contained, while each volume in the same situation is in a different intra-determination.

4. Undoubtedly, these various points may also to some extent cross-reference the several arguments advanced by sociologists or psychologists about the social construction of identity or personality. However, the objective and ultimate ambition of a theory of the volume cannot be dissociated from a micrological scale, with the aim of perceiving based on continuous micro-observations the gradual effects and traces left instant after instant by the actions, emotions and thoughts of the volume in question or those that other volumes left on this volume and his consistency, as well as those left by various events. Thus, I constantly refer to the issue of considering the volumic unity and its continuity as a point of reference for observations. It is from this perspective that the notion of anthropologicality seems relevant to me. It does not define a possible discourse, whether specific or general, on human condition, which derives from and depends on analyses of cultures or actions. Rather, it indicates a type of anthropology,

---

27 For example, in a recent article: [RAP 15].

which is literally anthropological because it reveals the human being, based on a description of his existence "step by step" and instant after instant, with a potentially variable and yet sufficiently precise focus. I employ the term "anthropologicality" by analogy with the word "literality", which indicates something in keeping with the "word for word" of a text. Such a description can give us a basic anthropologicality, which might be self-sufficient without at first requiring supplementary interpretations. Nonetheless, in so doing, this kind of practice, with its ambition, and accuracy and exhaustivity as its goals, remains partial and specific to each observer's eye and position – but this seems obvious to me – even if it can always be supplemented. As we keep saying that there are no raw data, we forget that some data are more raw than other data and, as it were, literal. Focusing on this basic anthropologicality, which, in my opinion, anthropology should not overlook, reveals the gap between the concrete step-by-step of humans and the themes that inform so-called anthropological research – a specific ritual in a given region of the world, a specific neighborhood in a city, handing down a technique, life in a given environment, etc. – and that yet cannot avoid an empirical, but sidestepped, confrontation with the continuity of the instants of human volumes. Thus, we can see clearly that anthropology has during its history suspended its basic principle. It is based on this principle that I find it important for anthropology to consider or reconsider its specificity as a field of study with a potential diversity of applications, which should undoubtedly be invented, and an awareness of the boundaries beyond which anthropologicality is lost, making way for sociological, ethnological or culturological research. An existantial type of anthropology gives me the hope that we will walk down this radical path.

5. I have repeated over and over again that a human volume is a separate body that is about to continue. This volume differs from any other volume, as he appears then visible to an observer and as he feels it more or less implicitly or explicitly. Therefore, I set down another consequence: the identity of a human volume cannot be defined only through the cognitive ability to recall acts that have been carried out and to recognize himself as a specific volume, or because others recognize him as such, but because a volume is a single empirical unity that can be monitored uninterruptedly and continuously, and because a sort of consistency pervades him and keeps him the same through changes hour after hour and over time. In any case, a cloned substitute would represent another volume, who would be separate and whose temporal and stylistic continuity would then differ from that of the original volume, in addition to the (minimal) genetic variations that may

occur during the embryonic process, as I have pointed out. Similarly, if cloning or any other process whereby a volume is copied involved a volume's destruction or aimed to replace him because he is dead, the new recreated volume would naturally be a different volume, even if he is identical or nearly identical to the first volume, as then he would be involved in a new type of continuity[28]. All this reveals that each human volume as such cannot be replaced. Presenting a volume as the first entity entails some consequences on everyone's ethical way of considering everyone else. In my opinion, this observation should be attentive and thorough, besides lucidly and simultaneously assessing each volume's singularity and separation[29]. For example, this would be equally important for potential psychotherapeutic approaches that imply the highlighting of volumic irreducibility beyond voluments, in particular perceptions of a lack of unity or identity or a feeling of discontinuity, which only represent modifiable perceptions of and within a volume. And this volume is indeed present.

1.5. Lessereity

1. Besides continuing coherence and pervading voluments, there is another key element in a human volume, which regulates the way he appropriates what happens. This is lessereity, which we have already identified in relation to obliqueness and passivity. What does it mean? When we observe a human being, we see that when he carries out an action with other humans, he does not do as much as we may think: being there and carrying out what has to be done, without significant mental and physical effort, by force of habit, with a parsimonious perception which may naturally change according to the situations, and even in those that might seem demanding. Most actions with others are carried out in a situation without any requirements other than something I have called "minimal joining behavior". Highly visible from the outside, what corresponds to the minimal joining behavior in a volume may be more or less shared by other volumes in the same situation with different degrees of likeness whether they are part of a military parade or sitting down in a subway train. I have already mentioned this point. The role fulfilled this way does not necessarily invade the immediate lived presence. These minimal behaviors are accomplished all the more easily when they are often-repeated acts or routines and when they

---

28 For these details, see [LEW 15].
29 I have already emphasized this point in previous works, in particular [PIE 17].

can resort to or rely on well-known rules or points of reference. Not only is this layer of shared voluments never strictly shared identically, as it is mixed with other voluments like social traces or style, but in addition, each volume adds in a different way to his minimal acts some peripheral gestures[30] and heterogeneous thoughts[31] in relation to the action in question, some detached gazes and an absence of the inner state that would have corresponded to these expected actions[32]. In a volume, lessereity, which has the effect of tempering what happens and avoiding a direct confrontation with an issue concerning an event, includes these leftovers, which may well be identified as such, but also and more globally these minimal expression that characterize human volumes. In addition to the integration of what happens through and within the consistency of a volume and his capacity to retain his acts, lessereity emerges as another intravolumic operative principle. Lessereity often includes details and leftovers or extra elements which, however, indicate something "less". There are countless examples everywhere.

1.1. Instant after instant, what is most surprising is not so much the daily obviousness of routines as the fact that it is never totally put on hold, even in the face of conflict, incongruity and tension, which are thereby lessened. A human volume is characterized by his way not only of mixing passivity with the tension involved in an action but also of not wanting to know, of being docile even as he leads a political revolution, of not drawing the consequences of an action and finding, even in situations that may seem extreme, supports and remaining points of reference that somehow ensure his continuity. Lessereity is a sort of diffuse reversibility that modulates other dimensions (such as responsibility, justification and rationality, which are always on the horizon) and makes it possible to lessen, transfer, move, postpone and not delimit the issue at the center of a word or act. At the very beginning of *Ecclesiastes*, we can read: "All the rivers run into the sea; yet the sea is not full; unto the place from whence the rivers come, thither they

---

30 In [PIE 17], I pointed out a large number of secondary gestures (see also [REM 03]).

31 However, these thoughts may become burdensome feelings, which are not necessarily visible and do not prevent the situation from unfolding smoothly.

32 In previous works, especially [PIE 96] and [PIE 15], I drew the attention to the fact that ethnographic processes of any kind must nearly unavoidably discard these details. If this is the case, it is because the goal of these types of research is not the human being, but collective wholes, or the human being conceived as part of a collective group. If the human volume were really the target of the observation methods, evidently this large number of details would figure in the description and analysis of the human.

return again." I would say the same about a human volume as he is approached by messages, events and beings. Therefore, lessereity organizes the voluments in a volume, making it possible to lessen the feeling of an action or emotion, or what other volumes send in the volume's direction, to "detach oneself" from others, to not think about the possible weight of the consequences of an action or emotion, to not feel this, to feel this less or to get rid of this at least in part.

1.2. This can be explained in different words. I have mentioned before the simultaneity of logics of action in one volume at a given time t. Therefore, it is possible to say that a volume represents always more than one logic of action. However, he represents always less than that as well. In my opinion, this is more important than the first aspect, and we often forget about it. Simultaneously, and not only in a volume, there are several logics of action involved, but at the same time each of these, for example, constraint, rationality, communication or strategy, does not follow its own logic as far it could. Thus, the lessereity that pervades logics of action does not let these so-called rational, communicational, practical or constraining actions, as well as some others, actually and totally be so. The voluments concerned are somehow lessened in the volume himself. Such forms of lessereity can be found: in what is left implicit or in the background, which includes, for example, the reasons for acting (Weber) and constraints (Durkheim) that are there without being there, as they are hardly perceived in the acts that succeed one another situation after situation; in a more or less reduced expression, namely that of Bourdieu's "social" sphere – I mean what we are all exposed to during our childhood, for example – which does not manifest itself wholly and simultaneously or every single time and which is not a copy of what has been received, as it combines with other voluments in a volume and is tempered by the traces of various trajectories or personal style; in the non-feeling or non-perception of this social sphere; in the leftovers that seep in and make the communication and comprehension of messages always partial:

> Just pay attention to sociable conversation! If the word isn't already dead by the time it reaches the other person, he immediately proceeds to murder it by contradictions, diversions, side-stepping and whatever else you like to call the thousand varieties of unmannerliness in conversation. [GOE 98, p. 88]

These words, written by Goethe, clearly show this "lessereity", especially if we are willing to remove the strategic dimension that can be associated with this "murder" or "unmannerliness". Such a lessereity will not necessarily represent the goal for conversational studies in ethnomethodology or Goffmanian analyses focusing on ways of speaking.

1.3. Virginia Woolf seems to lament how rare intense days "in being" are, adding that even these instants are drowned in "non-being", "in a kind of nondescript cotton wool" [WOO 02, p. 84]. She also points out that only few novelists can describe well [WOO 02, p. 84]. Could we say the same about the anthropologists or sociologists interested mainly in the issues concerning collective phenomena? "Non-being" is not secondary, and it may even be key for the presence of human volumes. Once again, an accurate observation of lessereity implies focusing on a volume in his entirety and continuity. The methodological consequence of continuity is essential if I want to discover what lessens the issue involved in a situation and in existence in general at all times. I do not think it is possible to identify lessereity properly and consider the actual extent of this "less" that takes place constantly and multiplies in the continuity of a volume if we observe groups or interactions.

2. It may be useful to name and distinguish between the various expressions of lessereity and, consequently, to grasp their diversity properly. These forms have nothing to do with daily tactics and other differences from role, and even less so with the more or less organized forms of social distance. Lessereity is more diffuse. Therefore, it is not associated with voluntary or dysfunctional attitudes. Rather, it is a lack of lessereity that creates burdens in the situations faced in life, as is shown by some types of mental health problems – however, if we pay attention, it is not a total lack of lessereity that characterizes them either. Naturally, at every moment, not all the voluments of a volume are necessarily concerned by lessereity, and especially by all its expressions, as specific expressions apply here and there to specific voluments and to some roles but not others. Indeed, I could say that lessereity is also a volument in the entirety of a volume. In any case, instant after instant, the expressions of lessereity described below accumulate, together with their ways of structuring the other voluments of a volume, and especially of decreasing the degree of intensity of an action or emotion. Lessereity works as a sort of intravolumic ratchet that holds back the deployment of acts in general, as do style, other pervading voluments, and the traces of the continuity of instants. These expressions are a key principle for the constitution of a volume. Here, I come across the

parameters used before to describe the density of presence, and I will clarify them again.

– Presence–absence: It defines a way of being active in a situation while also being on a lesser level, elsewhere, through thoughts, looks or gestures, absent-mindedly, distracted but only slightly so by external things. It results from a type of simultaneity between a main action and secondary actions (gestures or thoughts) which do not disrupt it, within the limits allowed by the situation and the tolerance involved[33]. I can distinguish between temporary distraction, based on a peripheral perception of contingent things, maximum-distraction, through which an individual emerges in a situation as if he were still involved in previous situations or already in other situations that will follow, and detachment, when there is no willing defensive strategy, through which an individual does not really become involved in a situation. The idea of minor mode often refers to these distinctive features.

– Incompletion: It can be found in actions and especially words that do not fully exploit their significance and are not taken all the way in terms of their intrinsic nature or reception of what happens. Therefore, these acts seem to stop, as if they turned around, remaining incomplete and occasionally deferred until a later time. They find no closure, they are not decisive and they do not extend their development. It is as if there were a ratchet leading to a U-turn or a stop before an act or word can continue.

– Hesitation: Although incompletion defines an action that is not fully carried out, hesitation concerns an action or a word that hardly begins. There are some hesitation and some kinds of stammering and first faltering steps, but there may also be a certain degree of tension. It is as if doubt seeped into the early stages before something can be carried out and our thoughts found it difficult to be made known and did not dare to express themselves, diminishing in their attempt to express themselves. An individual who acts seems then to turn around and withdraw into himself through his hesitating words but also extra gestures without any direct meaning and even occasionally clumsy.

– Break or suspension: It emerges when an action or word, once completed, entails no consequences or does not have the effect that its content or meaning would seem to imply, as if a break, a type of cut-off took

---

33 For this topic, see Georg Simmel's book [SIM 86, pp. 32–35].

shape beyond a situation, as if, taken away by the fluidity of the moments following one another, what has been said or done were immediately lessened, remaining "fenced off" as it is accomplished, without any connection with the acts which follow and continue.

– Fluidity: It indicates everyone's ability to continue situation after situation, even between situations that are regulated by roles, principles and values that may differ and even contradict one another. It is also involved when a volume tolerates or can barely see some contradictions that emerge around him. It is then a type of tolerance, in a situation, aimed at the elements that are not in keeping with what it implies. A similar case occurs when a volume, feeling the weight and emotion of his own contradictions, circumvents them. Habits may help, instant after instant, withdraw from nearly naturally, or even just a little, what happens, contradictions, imperfections and roles, and yet not as part of an explicitly critical approach. Thus, presence is dis-intensified, so that it becomes easier to move between situations. In this case, I think that fluidity seems more like a principle that concerns how a volume is held back than a flow with which the idea of flux is at first associated.

– Oblivion: The series of moments and situations following one another nearly naturally gives rise to some forgetfulness that manifests itself in at least three identifiable ways. On the one hand, at every moment, several actions, words and perceptions are immediately lost or in any case put aside. On the other hand, various acts and events that have not been forgotten nearly immediately can be forgotten gradually. Furthermore, several consequences, emotions, or affects, which could not be rapidly nuanced, but which may resurface, are also gradually dulled until they are buried. They are somehow relegated to the background.

– Hypolucidity: This is the term I use to refer to the way in which humans are situated in a non-consciousness, or in any case below even a minimum lucidity level, or to designate a way of not seeing and closing one's eyes, not really examining the issues and consequences related to what happens, but also not knowing one's own characteristics, including one's social or stylistic features. In a human volume, lucidity, knowledge, consciousness, sensitivity and emotions are, as it were, prevented from accentuating and focusing on a volument of the volume himself or of other volumes. Hypolucidity is less a type of distance from oneself than from specific voluments or elements of reality. Here, as it was the case for forgetfulness or fluidity, the distinguishing feature is a non-activation of these modes of consciousness as well as memories or emotions that could be centered on a specific action or another volument.

– Habits: They correspond to the pervading presence of types of knowledge or know-hows established in a volume, and they reduce the possible tensions related to gestures, thoughts or emotions. Habit is an effect of time. Thus, attentive actions and the emotions that had been felt at first turn into routines and automatic gestures, which require no attention, control or alertness, allow not to think about or verify everything, allow to trust and rely on the various supports provided by a situation, and therefore create a flexible rhythm or even some sort of detachment in the interrelated series of actions and thoughts. Style itself is a form of habit that makes some choices, decisions and actions less burdensome.

– Docility: It refers to the fact of accepting what can be found or what happens in a situation without the desire or will to change anything. Docility is often associated with habits, know-hows or reasons behind a specific action, and it will involve a routine and the implicit use of rules and various points of reference and clues that can make it easier to lower one's guard. Therefore, based on this minimal perception, docility allows actions and social roles to be easily carried out and taken on respectively time and again[34].

3. Lessereity is the very sign that there are human volumes, who are different and separate from one another. This is the element evoked by this "less": the fact that each volume remains separate from the others and from the collective stakes of a situation as he withdraws into himself in several ways. On the one hand, some detached or present–absent attitudes in particular reveal that humans cannot fully establish links, carry out actions or send messages. These attitudes involve, in a diffuse and implicit manner, a sort of renunciation (we know that we cannot really cross the bridge that separates us), distance (e.g. from someone else, who does not really listen to me) and indifference (about an incomplete link, which is flawed in several senses), so that actions involving others can seem less difficult or imperfect.

---

34 Apart from these forms, playing represents a way of introducing reserve and some distance, which is, however, explicit and voluntary, from a role, an action, a word and a social or cultural mark. Like a child pretending to be a cowboy, everyone can reveal a more or less significant gap in relation to an expected behavior. Into this gap seep humor, irony, some forms of guile, and occasionally excess, which can indicate a type of distance.

However, on the other hand, besides these attitudes, lessereity is, at the heart of the presence of the human volume, a fundamental principle. In my opinion, there are no humans without this "less". In fact, lessereity is inherent in the volumic principle, in its unity and uniqueness, in the impossibility of eluding this unity, and, therefore, in its ways of managing what happens. As he develops an intrinsically unitary way of being, a volume, in addition to the pervading voluments and style in particular, resorts to the expressions of lessereity in his appropriation, strictly speaking, of external events, messages and emotions within the volumic unity itself. Rays, even as attempts, sent or received, do leave traces and effects which can then accumulate, as we have seen. A volume works like a type of unity that always tends to turn back on itself, regulating through lessereity what is added to it or what modifies a specific volument. Therefore, a volume forgets, does not see, does not want to see, accepts, stops thinking about it, relies on certain things and continues. In this case, his appropriation is lessening. Because of it, what happens is or remains specific to oneself or, as it were, to the volume and to one's volume. This is also the case when a volume may, or wants to, be led here and there by the perceived intensity of messages and emotions which, based on how open he can be, he will express or receive, but which will also be lessened in several ways by the expressions of lessereity. With style and the various social marks established in a volume, appropriation is a "positive" way of characterizing him, and of holding him back, of retaining him. It complements the effect created by lessereity which, however, is a type of appropriation that takes place through a "reduction", a distance that is "negative", as it were, deriving from a volume who remains in his unity. Thus, this is another way in which what emerges from one's own volume is regulated, as if a filling or excessive filling process could threaten the volume himself.

3.1. Inherent in a volume, lessereity is not something that should be put aside or a loss that should be avoided, so that a volume manages to appropriate in a more "authentic" way or succeeds in being "himself" and in carrying out "his" conquest or recovery of himself, as Heidegger may suggest [HEI 10, p. 162]. What I mean to say is that lessereity is straightaway an appropriation. It is an operative principle for the individual as he is an individual, one and separate, and because he cannot be otherwise regardless of what he does or thinks. Lessereity ensures and protects a volume and his singularity. It is as if it defended the volumic unity. Therefore, it lessens actions and emotions, as various traces take shape. In this way as well, the consistency and continuity of a volume prevail over words or acts that emerge and can of course have consequences. They thus prevail over the various types of "otherness" that occur but are lessened in one way or another. Style itself, like social or cultural traces, may be lessened, combined with other voluments, as only some traits manifest themselves, and not necessarily be felt, just as lessereity is pervaded by style. Should a volume be clearly aware of a specific expression of lessereity – this awareness may also be marked by a stylistic expression or a social trace – then this would continue causing what lessereity contributes to, namely a volume's withdrawal into himself. This does not preclude other lessening traits in a volume. According to Lévinas' expressions, which can easily apply to a volume, once this volume has "a basis", he "gathers [him]self together", but does this mean that he "stands up and masters all that encumbers [him]", as he notes just after [LEV 78, p. 71]? As if he could not get rid of the vocabulary of action, when he considers rest and this basis, Lévinas considers the "activity of inactivity" [LEV 78, pp. 35–36] to indicate that at the very heart of inactivity or rest there is an act: "it is the act of positing oneself on ground, it is rest inasmuch as rest is not a pure negation but this very tension of a position, the bringing about of a *here*" [LEV 78, p. 36]. What I can see above all in a volume is a type of inactivity of, or rather in activity.

3.2. Lessereity is a highly intravolumic principle. Thus, I think that there is a gap between the unity of a volume, as I am trying to describe it, which is naturally not closed and includes various voluments, and a form of altercentrism that characterizes in different ways the anthropological tradition and can also be seen in various discourses that highlight, for example, how in everyone there is a part of others. However, the other in each volume is especially effects and traces of voluments, and more precisely effects lessened in the volumic unity. The possibility of being altered and feeling oneself transformed at a given time by an event or a word is associated with a possibility of "disaltering", which may be more or less rapid or gradual. I think that this is essential for any description or understanding of a human volume. This volume contains a part of indifference to what happens, in particular to others, whereas he is intrinsically not indifferent to himself. Someone indifferent is not concerned about the characteristic of something and does not see any difference. He lessens and appropriates in various ways. This is a permanent dimension in the presence of a human volume. However, a volume is not indifferent to himself or his unity based on the very way in which he goes on. Thus, a volume remains united while also being separate, detaching himself from what happens, but also appropriating and remaining this way with others. Therefore, this allows the lessening human being to be with others without worrying about the limits inherent in so-called collective life. This point recalls another: sociology, including social anthropology, should understand the types of collective life, and existantial anthropology should understand how a volume works as such, as a separate volume and permanently "dis-linked", marked, with lessereity, by a characteristic de-relational principle[35]. This is a structural and not a situational principle or something that emerges temporarily according to the circumstances.

4. Let us mention one last point. Paul Valéry wrote: "like a pure sound or a melodic system of pure sounds in the midst of noises, so a crystal, a flower, a sea shell stand out from the common disorder of perceptible things" [VAL 77, p. 112]. Likewise, the human being can be considered as a volume, looked at and observed in his continuity. It is important to mention that the features pointed out in the previous pages are real, concrete and can be observed in the forms of presence of a volume. As I aim for an anthropological science of this kind, could I go further in a search for laws and precise regularities in what constitutes a human volume: the organization of his voluments, what he integrates, how he integrates it, his capacity of lessereity, the role of details? In any case, always integrating these aspects into the entire volume would remain an essential condition. This chapter has tried to lay some conceptual foundations and therefore to suggest some modes of observing with this objective. We need to observe and describe human volumes considered as such in order to acquire a reasonable amount of knowledge. Hans Blumemberg expresses powerfully what a theory is as well as the need for lateral thinking. A theoretician is someone who sees less and less, as if he were working in "enclosures", as Blumemberg writes, with a limited exposure to the "outside world" [BLU 00, p. 1]. Naturally, the author of a theory is aware that he is ignorant, "but in the knowledge of what he does not know he is badly informed. Otherwise he would not be so fundamentally deficient in life's realism" [BLU 00, p. 9], hence, as Blumemberg emphasizes, the importance of "a shift in the direction of attention: drawing notice to the unnoticed" [BLU 00, p. 21]. Thus, volumology aims to look at a human volume and, afterwards, to keep looking at him more precisely, and so on. It is all a matter of details.

---

35 There are few works on detachment in anthropology (see [CAN 15]).

Illustrating: Drawings of Theory

2.1. Drawings and contraspective

1. Looking at a human being in continuity, moment after moment, may help us focus more on the being himself than on his connection with the situation, the environment, objects and other human beings. This is one of the things I learned from the film shot by Catherine Beaugrand and Samuel Dématraz, which was focused on me uninterruptedly for nearly 12 hours. Observing and re-observing some images excerpted from a movie of this kind undoubtedly helps us become aware of the reality of a human volume [PIE 17]. It is as if continuous observation helped us look at a volume, which consequently remains foregrounded as the central figure, leaving the context in the background. This method plays an important role in discovering the human being as the "object" of anthropology.

2. Putting the volume of being in the foreground as he stands out from his context, looking at him, observing him specifically, regarding him as separate from the others, conceiving him entirely rather than as reduced to some fragments and thinking about him with his details and incompletion: the characteristics and concepts introduced above may naturally be theoretically autonomous. However, in order to make this material clear and instructive, I can hardly dissociate my theoretical arguments from a set of drawings. I drew the first few by chance on a board in front of my students. They now seem to me a significant element or even nearly a necessity in this process which involves writing and developing the ideas elaborated about the volume of being. Thus, these drawings represent fully fledged mediums of this theory. They strengthen the heuristic power of the uninterrupted film in order to help me see human beings.

2.1. Henri Michaux writes that drawing means capturing beings not through words but through "graphic signs" [MIC 01, p. 12]. He wishes to "draw the consciousness of existing and the flow of time" , and the goal is "to draw the moments that little by little make up life, to let people see the phrase within, the phrase without words, a rope indefinitely unrolling, winding, accompanying in its intimacy all that comes in from the outside, and the inside, too" [MIC 97, p. 320]. This comparison cannot hold, especially if we want to look at Michaux's drawings and simultaneously read his words. In reality, it is less movement or flow than the human volume himself that drives me to draw in order to supplement the concepts used to analyze the volume of being.

2.1.1. The history of photography is controversial in the social sciences or, in any case, it has to face limited uses that are not really acknowledged as tools in their own right, even if we can recognize (and discuss too) its objectifying or indexical value, because of the light imprint that photography leaves on what a photographer wishes to capture. This debate concerned the first anthropological attempts to study "human races" and search for their distinguishing features. Étienne Serres, who was Professor of Anatomy at the Museum of Natural History in Paris around 1850, established that photography could reproduce faithfully, and drawings merely provided a representation, as they were part of an artistic act and the personality of the artist permeated them too deeply: "In most cases art shines in it more brightly than reality. Now, it is this reality, naked and artless as it is, that a daguerreotype provides us, so that this gives an otherwise irreplaceable certainty to the figures thereby obtained" (quoted in [DIA 94, pp. 43–44]). However, during the same period, Broca thought that drawings were able to nuance, and, in order to avoid imprecisions, he devised "chromatic scales", for example 20 kinds of eye colors and more for skin and hair in order to render these nuances and, on this basis, measure averages and quantities [DIA 94, p. 45].

2.1.2. The epistemological properties of a photographic image guided a significant part of my work several years ago [PIE 92, PIE 10]. Tracing silhouettes, drawn on tracing paper placed on a photograph, came afterward. This operation can create a sort of filter from images cluttered with details, but it simultaneously allowed me to bring out human presences and volumes – even though I did not use this term at the time – with their various layers, which were represented by lines of varying thickness: relevant elements and other less pertinent elements, the particular details of an action and its expected elements.

2.1.3. When I had to publish some photographs of festive parades and the outlines of some silhouettes, I did not hesitate, as if it were self-evident that the photographs taken by an anthropologist can aim only to show things that are not visible to the naked eye or answer the questions that I wanted to ask the photographs. As the following drawings were due for publication, I did have some doubts, as if I did not feel authorized to draw and felt I was not skilled in this activity, maybe because I remembered the poor grades I received back in school. Besides, I have no objections if these drawings are called sketches or drafts.

2.2. The drawings presented here do not aim to represent anyone in particular. As drawings of theory, they cannot be separated from my theory. I draw them based on my knowledge of what the idea of a human volume implies, guided by my way of conceiving him, and with the aim of bringing out more clearly the anthropology of the volume. Thus, these drawings illustrate. I am not using this verb in the usual sense of providing images but in its strong etymological meaning, which in Latin means "clarifying", "shedding light on", and "making evident". Therefore, these drawings aim to shed light on the analysis of the human volume, clarify theoretical principles and better understand what a volume is and what constitutes one.

2.2.1. These drawings were not drawn in the field, for example in a field notebook, as Michael Taussig does, wisely recalling the other meanings of "to draw": to pull a thread as if to undo a knot, as water can be drawn from a well, or to be drawn to someone or something [TAU 11, p. XII]. Thus, I could say that drawing makes it possible to draw a volume from where he is situated: relegated to the background of perspectives which have lost him and cannot see him or theoretical constructs that have dissolved him in favor of other things. In fact, a drawing allows me to remain drawn by and to the volume I draw. Vocabulary often help us shed light on the matter, and this applies to the French word *trait* (which also means a line). It comes from the Latin verb *trahere* and may refer to the furrows left by a plow. As Jacqueline Sudaka-Bénazéraf points out, there is a literal meaning, which refers to a cut, a slit in the ground or on paper and also a figurative meaning that defines a prominent feature, a highlight and its opposite, that is, deletion, as in the French expression *tirer un trait* ("to draw a line" under something) [SUD 08, p. 12]. A drawing pulls, splits and highlights. It also erases what we do not wish to show.

2.2.2. Therefore, the drawings below do not result from an inner instinct that guides the pencil. On the contrary, as I am drawing, I can sense the presence of my conceptual analysis, which guides the lines. Besides, this resonates with the history of the word "drawing" in French, that is, *dessin*:

> Until the eighteenth century, the act of drawing, *dessiner*, was synonymous with a project or an intention, and the same word – *dessein* – was employed to refer to both. Drawings were at the time subordinate to the other arts, painting, sculpting, architecture, and merely regarded as a preliminary step for a work. [BAU 15, p. 2]

In my case, drawing is a step in an anthropological approach to the human being. Therefore, I draw by controlling the lines precisely in order to shed more light on and render more visible a volume whom I conceive mentally in some of his characteristics before the very act of drawing. Occasionally, in so doing, a drawing allows me to point out or nuance my own initial idea and encourages a written explanation. If we think about it, what is important is not so much the lines traced in a drawing, which is ever moving and never completed, as Tim Ingold [ING 13a] would say, but rather the volume represented, given that the issue is to conceive the consistency or density of a human being, namely not only movement but also stabilized elements, precisely a volume of being.

2.2.3. I will add that I do not use drawings to point out that the reality of a human being depends on the observer's perspective, but, on the contrary, I suggest that this reality is independent, according to the idea that a drawing encourages us to be surprised by this and say: "Did you see, the human being; there are human beings!" The issue is not to represent in drawings what may resemble imagination or the invisible, but to represent real things, even if at times these involve hardly perceptible details. Furthermore, my drawings are not destined to be directly collaborative and to invite immediate reactions from the individuals drawn[1].

---

1 Interested readers may refer to a general article on the resurgence of drawings in anthropology [TON n.d.]. This article showed me that my use of drawings is marked by a group of characteristics that often differ from those mentioned by the author concerning the recent approaches in the social sciences that resort to drawings.

3. Ultimately, and this point is significant, drawings allow me to criticize ethnography as a field of study focused on links and relations and to reveal the relevance of an emphasis on the human being rather than on interactions or relations in general. Looking at a human being means looking at him and nothing else, as I have said. This is not easy, and by avoiding this difficulty it opens the door to all sorts of thoughts on things other than human beings: environments, societies, relations and actions. In other words, looking at a human being is the opposite of putting into perspective, an act to which observers are used. "*Perspectiva* is a Latin word which means 'seeing through'. This is how Dürer sought to explain the concept of perspective" [PAN 91, p. 27]. Panofsky begins his book about "perspective as symbolic form" with this reference. When making a link between ethnographic operations and perspective, it is the meaning "to see through" that applies much more than the other possible meaning of the Latin *perspicere*: "to see clearly" [PAN 91, p. 75]. I think that the idea of "through" expresses aptly what a perspective implies. Looking through naturally means looking at human beings but especially, on the one hand, crossing them and going through to focus on something beyond them and, on the other hand, regarding this "beyond" as the central point that pushes human beings to the background.

3.1. In the history of painting, the expression of perspective is complex and multifaceted. However, what Panofsky writes about the topic may raise questions for an ethnographer:

> "The ultimate basis of the homogeneity of geometric space is that all its elements, the 'points' which are joined in it, are mere determinations of position, possessing no independent content of their own outside of this relation, this position which they occupy in relation to each other. Their reality is exhausted in their reciprocal relation: it is a purely functional and not a substantial reality. Because fundamentally these points are devoid of all content, because they have become mere expressions of ideal relations, they can raise no question of a diversity in content. Their homogeneity signifies nothing other than this similarity of structure" [PAN 91, p. 30].

Involved in the narrative dynamics of perspective, according to Merleau-Ponty's words, faces are "always subordinated to a character, a passion, or a mood – always signifying" [MER 73, p. 53]. I indeed refer to a general idea of "perspective" beyond its variations, including the theoretical ones, and what it has implied in the history of painting. In any case, perspective may be presented as a way of placing individuals and objects on a surface. A painting is then read as a visual path that connects places and above all characters that seem to be moving, about to go somewhere and act in a story. It is therefore considered as "a space where logical and narrative relations become visible" [ARA 08, p. 216]. Thus, and this seems very important to me, perspective does not involve facing a being, since it always strives to go beyond him, go through him and establish relations between different human beings. It is a way of representing the "being in the world", whom I critique page after page and to whom the volume himself cannot be reduced. Perspective helps me then question the loss of the entire volume, thus reduced to a narrative position. Beyond the possible illusion of "make pretend", perspective as a device confronts us, perhaps more than any other representation, with the loss of density of the individuals or objects represented. This is the case because "in a painting, things do not appear as they really are, they are a sign, they represent, and therefore what we wished to capture, the essential content of our presence in the world, disappears" [HAM 07, p. 49]. Another point follows: representing in perspective space and figures allows us to consider a painting as something made by and for someone. Of course, this may open a "rift" in the so-called "humanist" culture and provoke another reduction, that of the human being, "to an eye and this eye to a point" [DAM 00, p. 45], but it may also cause what is represented to be less significant than a painter or spectator's view, which is then somehow abandoned to the view of one or the other. Perspective as a device, therefore, sheds light on the operation highlighted in the social sciences and ethnography in particular: on the one hand, the reduction of beings to relational dynamics and narrative expressions and, on the other hand, a tendency to overlook them in favor of the observer's point of view with his specific features.

3.1.1. Thus, as I read a little about perspective as a device, I naturally think about ethnography and its specific modalities of observation and writing. Ethnography pertains to perspective as a "symbolic form", namely as a way of grasping the world, "a specific feeling of the metamorphosis of the perceptive space", which finds expression according to Panofsky both in artists and in philosophers or scientists [PAN 76, p. 93]. Structure, creation of relations, loss of human volumes – to different degrees, ethnographic results are not dissimilar from the perspective used as a device in painting, as I see it. In fact, an ethnographer, who looks, takes notes, looks again, describes, analyzes and conceptualizes, puts beings into culture, group and society, and, if he adopts a critical attitude towards these "perspectives", he cannot avoid putting beings into relation and interaction, but also creating affection dynamics between himself and what he is trying to understand. Regardless of the ethnographer's point of view and how he puts into perspective (in culture or in action) he experiences tens and hundreds of situations when carrying out so-called "fieldwork". These are a series of space-time contexts in which he observes, talks and takes notes. It is as if , at the very moment of looking and/or writing, he "passed through" the humans, retaining only the features he deems relevant for his perspective and his ultimate "target". It is this target that becomes the foreground, in front of the humans. It is as if this perspective sucked humans in, reduced them, and gradually lost them along the path it creates towards the horizon.

3.1.2. In Latin, *contra* means "in front, face-to-face". Looking and describing a volume implies, in reality, blocking perspective, focusing one's view and writing in a "contraspective". Naturally, the volumographic exercise is not a "face-to-face" exercise. Yet, it is a focused and radical look of a human being aims not to go through him. The observer tends to keep facing the volume or standing beside him, just as he moves with him and keeps him on the same scale throughout the observation and description process. Unlike perspective, contraspective no longer involves looking through and beyond but focusing on the volume himself, carrying out this action until the final draft. In French, the verb *volumer* means "putting in a volume, writing" [GOD 03, p. 626]. Thus, contraspective involves "voluming", namely presenting the human figure as entire and singularized as well as detaching it from the background, bringing it into relief without losing it in the various kinds of perspectives. Voluming implies moving away from what occasionally characterizes portraits and takes precedence in the narrative. In painting, like in ethnography, a portrait often presents an individual in his social context, as representative of a professional category and cultural identity, as involved in a specific event, and a symbol of a trajectory or specific social situation. Voluming thus means releasing the volume from his contexts. Yet, it is still possible to identify on his surface or in his content something that may be traditionally understood as part of the background. But voluming means mostly adding, continuing to add details of the volume as he is considered attentively. Voluming means also following the volume over a given period of time as he moves, without absorbing him into a narrative or a story. Voluming thus means indicating a way in which the volume withdraws from the narrative logic and resists links and relations.

3.2. Here, drawing a human being makes all his critical and heuristic force felt. As a vehicle for thinking, the drawing establishes, brings about, and imposes a direct confrontation with a volume, and, as in its attempt to represent him, it does not allow us to move past him. Drawing a human volume becomes a radical critique of perspective. It is as if the act of drawing could not adopt a perspective or go beyond the being represented. It is in Paul Valéry's comments that I perceived the clearest expression of this possible consequence entailed by drawing and the deliberate attention it implies in the act itself. "There is an immense difference between seeing a thing without a pencil in the hand and seeing it while drawing it" [VAL 60, p. 36]. Making the effort to draw a being makes us become aware that we have never really seen one. However, and most importantly, this type of drawing implies wakefulness, as Valéry says, and a new focus on the being. Thus, as he explains, we can see that we only used our eye as an "intermediary" to speak and think about other things. "The act of drawing a given object endows the eye with a power of command which must be sustained by the will [...] The end and the means of this willed seeing is the drawing itself" [VAL 60, p. 36]. I could say that a drawing of this kind is a contraspective act. Thus, drawing a volume involves, necessarily, not looking through or thinking beyond. It concretizes this contraspective.

2.2. Focusing on the human figure

Most drawings were drawn with felt-tip pens of different sizes. Some were drawn with pencils. This process took a little over a year, with a significant concentration of drawings in January 2017 when I began. Often, human beings are represented from the side in order to mark more easily their gestures as well as what happens from outside. It is my limited skills that did not allow me to represent these humans as three-dimensional volumes. In my opinion, their heuristic and instructive quality is not affected. For a long time, I considered to incorporating these drawings into the theoretical part about the volume in Chapter 1. I ultimately decided to include a specific chapter, between the theory of the volume and the theoretical debates of the following two chapters, to provide the possibility of moving back and forth between some elements of the theoretical part and these drawings.

2.2.1. *Putting into perspective*

Putting into perspective means transporting human beings into stories and contexts. This involves removing, as this drawing suggests, the human being and relegating him to the background: it is like a game.

If put into perspective, human volumes shrink and become gradually smaller (left). They are progressively less visible – their lines become increasingly less thick, from left to right and upwards (right). Therefore, I want to point out that these volumes become less and less important for an observer. As he keeps investigating, the observer focuses less on them. He looks for other things. At times, the volumes fade and are nearly eliminated in favor of another entity, for example a collective entity.

Looking at a human volume implies accepting that we cannot see or that we can hardly see the other volumes and entities involved in a situation. If we look without adopting a perspective (according to the meaning developed above), a volume remains central and in the foreground of the drawing, in gray, while beside him there are other smaller human beings drawn with finer lines and a hardly visible context that includes trees and buildings. On the other hand, in the background of the drawing, the use of perspective causes the volume as the entity observed to be put on hold or into parentheses, as the groups of volumes, the contexts and the environments become the elements prioritized in the analysis. What was subordinate to the foreground (the others, buildings and trees) becomes the central element. In turn, these are filled with gray.

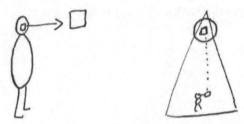

Fragmentation involves extracting a volument, which is presented as central for the observer. This volument is then put into perspective in relation to a social situation. It is on this level that the analysis is carried out. The volume will be forgotten, as he has become secondary or is even absent.

Turning anthropology into a science that focuses on human volumes means prioritizing the human figure and no longer the background as a "sucking" mechanism. Focusing on a volume, filming him and zooming in on him means that the context, other volumes and the environment become secondary. This is why, naturally, the lines of the central volume are more marked, so that he can stand out from the situational context.

2.2.2. *Separation*

Human volumes are separate (left). They have no arms or facial expressions, so that their separation can somehow appear more clearly. They can get closer and occasionally touch one another or attempt to touch or reach one another (right). Let us recall what Rilke writes about those individuals who "try to reach each other with words and gestures" [RIL 09, X]. I thought about this point also when I discovered, for example, some drawings that decorated medieval manuscripts: distinct beings who stretch their arms and seem to try to touch or speak to one another. However, they remain separate entities. There is an empty blank space that may be wide or narrow between them.

When volumes touch one another, their outline remains well defined.

2.2.3. *Focusing on the volume*

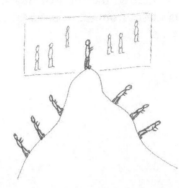

The volume observed is the one whose outline is drawn in bold, rather than the other individuals with whom he is involved in a situation (the rectangle). He is observed and followed as he continues on from other situations and moments and soon in other situations and moments.

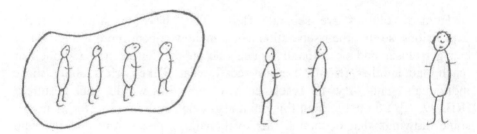

Looking at a volume does not mean looking at a group of volumes (left) or considering an interaction among volumes (center) but looking at only one volume at a time (right).

A volume meets another volume. Focusing on a volume (left) does not mean getting interested in their interaction (center). It also does not imply becoming interested in the human being as he interacts or in the human beings interacting, namely in the relevant lines for this interaction (right). The circle shows the elements considered by analyses that focus on interactions. They leave out a part of each volume in question.

A volume is about to act: he is holding a glass. Focusing on this volume in his entirety (left) does not mean focusing on the volume who is holding something as he is holding something (center) or on the object held (right). The lines in bold reveal the focus, which varies in each of these three cases.

A focus on the act of giving–receiving or the object given–received (the glass at the bottom) differs from a focus (right) on the entire volume as he intends to give something, and whose gesture is merely one of his constitutive elements.

2.2.4. *Rays*

A human being sends rays from every part of his volume. Whether they have a target or not, they move towards other volumes and thus progressively lose intensity – as shown by the black shading. The lines of the rays sometimes split, indicating that it will not be necessarily the same parts that move towards the other volumes.

Some rays (the starting point is indicated by the black circle) have a target or will reach a volume, but this volume is somehow protected from what happens to him and receives it in an attenuated form (as shown by the gray cloud). Things happen obliquely and laterally, below the intensity of their starting point, but this is enough to affect a volume. These intensities are absorbed and integrated into the volume (as also shown by the gray cloud).

A volume's arm points at a target and simultaneously turns back on the volume himself. This does not mean that rays do not continue towards other volumes (as shown by the gray cloud). This illustrates the etymology of the word "relation", which has been mentioned previously in this book. Saying or doing something somehow returns to the volume who says or does something.

2.2.5. *Voluments*

A volume is a compresence of different voluments, a role that he takes on at a given time t, some buried emotions, social and cultural traces and various habits. Therefore, various voluments permeate a specific action. Other voluments are put on hold, and they may or may not leave minimal traces.

In a volume, there are more or less permanent voluments that include knowledge, know-hows and ways of doing or saying something (the hatched gray section in the drawing on the left). There are other voluments, emotions and thoughts associated with a situation, according to which a volume may feel more or less "full" (in black in the same drawing). These thoughts or emotions can spill out of the volume more or less quickly (the drawing in the center) and leave a trace (the drawing on the right, the narrow black section). In the reality of the volume, voluments include various compresent elements that cannot necessarily be pinpointed and delimited. They are not layers horizontally placed on top of one another. However, this could be a heuristic approach used to represent the volume and what takes place in him.

The volume contains know-hows or various capacities (the small circle in the drawing on the left). These take concrete shape in situations by filling a part of the volume (the larger circle in the center drawing). After this moment, a trace may be left in the potential stock, which as a result is slightly modified (the drawing on the right, with the very small black dot above the circle).

2.2.6. *Consistency and style*

What is modified in a volumic consistency? Gestures take place (the first three drawings), an idea emerges as the moments follow one another (the third drawing), this idea weakens (the fourth drawing) and the consistency of the volume is not modified or is only hardly altered.

A volume contains various voluments with different elements (shown by the black and gray shading), but the whole is held together. The volume is represented without his legs in order to show more clearly his "foundation".

A volume retains through his consistency the action pervaded by styles, habits, social and cultural marks, and the role in progress.

Based on the same volument shared with other volumes (shown by the light gray area drawn in F pencil), the mark of a specific style (the circle in the center drawn in B or 8B pencil) leads to two different colors, which can be immediately identified in the volumes.

2.2.7. Volugrams

Apollinaire's "calligrams" are poems whose graphic arrangement constitutes a drawing. The word is a portmanteau combining *gramma*, which in Greek means letter or written signs, and *kallos*, which means beautiful. Therefore, "volugrams" may combine usual written signs, that is, words, with the visual representation of a volume, like the outline above, in order to indicate that actions, the social dimension and feelings do not go out of the volume and are voluments in a volume. Different typographical forms (uppercase or lowercase letters, italics, etc.) can distinguish the voluments: the main actions, their peripheral gestures, the traces of the "social" dimension and style, and feelings. I think I should point out that, in this case, it is not words that constitute a drawing. Rather, the drawing precedes the words written within it, just as a volume exists before carrying out a specific action and as he moves on from another situation, carrying various voluments: a know-how, habits, ideas, etc. My aim here is merely to suggest and outline a type of volumographic description. It is possible to invent other ways of representing the consistency and continuity of a volume over a more or less long period of time. The uninterrupted description in *Le Volume humain*, based on a continuous film that lasted 11 hours and 36 minutes and focused on a day in my life, totals 134 pages dedicated to the successions of acts. In another part, I have added feelings and various comments. I think that this type of description, like most, has the drawback of emphasizing actions too much and overlooking the consistency and continuity of the volume. This is why I am trying to find a graphic and typographical way of showing a volume and his unity beyond his actions, attempting then to clearly mark his importance relative to actions, which are secondary to the volume[2].

2.2.8. *Peripheral gestures, presence and absence*

A volume simultaneously does something and looks at something else. Distraction is a way of attenuating his presence as the action is in progress,

---

2 In the above volugram, I have only indicated a few actions (to drink, to take, to swallow, to eat, to look at, to walk, to look at again, to be sitting down, to read, to write, to talk, etc.) and this or that mood and thought. The volugram is of course to be completed.

unless the action is compromised. A volume acts and directs actions and words while also looking in another direction, letting his mind wander and letting a part of him turn back to him, as is shown by the arm movement.

A human volume speaks, sees, hears, looks, listens, is heard, is listened to, is seen and is looked at, but his acts do not take over the whole volume, that is, his and the others. This is what the white part of the drawing shows.

The volume contains voluments that may correspond to various logics of action, which are standard in the social sciences (communication, constraint, rationality, accomplishment, etc.). At a given time t, they may add up in a volume while also leaving some empty space (the drawing above). However, as the drawing on the right reveals, no logic is itself complete, as it is pervaded by some empty space or something negative.

The same volume lessens in the action he carries out and his way of being present. This is the same volume who shrinks as he does and says something, as this is in progress.

At the same moment, a volume does or says something while also folding in on himself, as if he could not bring his action to completion and protected himself from the others. This withdrawal into himself, illustrated by the gradual movement of the head back towards the body, can be hardly perceived in most cases. Besides, it may be more or less felt and more or less diffuse or explicit.

It emerges from all this that the human volume is not involved in reality from merely one point of view. An individual is not reduced to a point of view. He also has a point of "dis-view" that indicates his self-withdrawal. This drawing shows a part advancing and another receding, but within the volume himself. We should understand that this permanent retreat, which takes place as the volume is involved in a situation, does not leave the volume and is not necessarily problematic or a type of imbalance. On the contrary, it is as if the volume interrupted his perspective about the world through a dis-perspective, which is refocused onto himself.

Separation does not imply loneliness. It is accentuated here by the sitting position, the tilted torso and the face, which is increasingly folding back on the body, as is shown by the head movements (left). In any case, there is a part of non-communication in each volume. Lucidity of loneliness, separation or the ephemeral nature of the volume, represented here by eyes that seem somewhat bigger (right), is a state that is immediately lessened by human beings, who turn it into hypolucidity. Is this the view favored by the anthropologist?

3

Debates: Anthropology and the Human Entity

As Malinowski writes:

> First of all, it has to be laid down that we have to study here stereotyped manners of thinking and feeling. As sociologists, we are not interested in what A or B may feel *qua* individuals, in the accidental course of their own personal experiences – we are interested only in what they feel and think *qua* members of a given community. [MAL 22, p. 23]

These words are well known. They clearly reveal the intrinsically sociological dimension of the history of social and cultural anthropology. These volumes gathered together with the aim of understanding that a "human community" do not naturally allow us to understand a human being, unless we make him correspond exclusively to what he shares with others in a cultural group. This is the opposite of my intention here. Such anthropological approaches remain the most common[1]. Simultaneously, these points of view are regularly criticized. However, I would say that it is possible to level various criticisms at some branches of anthropology that have themselves been critical of the culturalist or sociological foundations of anthropology and that have explicitly focused on individuals and subjectivities without, however, truly considering the human being. In various ways, they have let him become fragmented and diluted in contexts

---

1 I would like to mention my critique of this Malinowskian point of view and cultural ethnography in [PIE 96, PIE 15, pp. 22–26].

and even homogenized with other humans. It is contemporary works of this kind that worry me[2]. When confronted with these types of research, which attempt to observe and describe in particular experience or existence, I have always felt some opposition on my part. I think that presenting the human being as a volume and as an entirety who is highlighted and stands out from the contextual background that surrounds him is very useful to understand my awkwardness towards anthropologists who challenge analyses in terms of culture, groups or representations and, based in part on phenomenology, target subjectivities themselves. In this chapter, I will mention some (but not all) anthropologists or anthropological trends that favor approaches in terms of existence and experience, or work and think starting from the individual, and also some philosophers whose ideas have shed or are shedding light directly on anthropology. Thus, I will see what becomes of the human volume as I freely jump from one author to another and from one approach to another, as if I were debating with each of them. Each time and according to different types of debates (with a school of thought, for example phenomenological or existential anthropology, or with an author and his ideas, for example Tim Ingold or Christina Toren), some critical elements will emerge and, as I hope, clarify my argument. As for the philosophers in question, especially Husserl, Heidegger, Merleau-Ponty, Sartre and Deleuze, it seems pointless to think that something new can be added to their combined ideas. Undoubtedly, based on their works, it may even be possible to create some profiles of volumes, just to deduce then more easily the missing elements of each reading. I will only mention some sensitive issues that may prevent a focus on the human being. Several points will emerge and re-emerge from these debates: the fragmentation of the volume, namely his reduction to some fragments, the reference to social contexts, the issue of relations, the role of philosophy, methodological questions and the level of detail. The volume will remain the central theme. I have divided this debate into topics: experience and existence, going beyond, wrenching and eccentricity, lines and flow, intersubjectivity and "perspections" of the individual, which represent as many forms of circumventing the human being. Readers should not expect a thorough epistemological analysis of these starting points. Above all, I want to show how such conceptual, theoretical and methodological frameworks do not necessarily grasp the volume and run the risk of overlooking him in one way or another. Naturally, I do not mean to challenge the work of a specific author, whose goal may not necessarily be to focus on the human being, let alone the work of authors with whom I have conversed or am still conversing, who

---

2 Naturally, I will not include here the research on the individual or singularity as representation or attribution categories.

have made me think about the difficulty involved in looking at a human being, and who may have changed their ideas themselves. Therefore, I present stages and expressions of thoughts that question me and help me build on my own thread and clarify it. In particular, what I intend to do is to start a discussion in which the focus is on the human being and the question asked is the following: how have anthropologists treated, and how do they intend to treat, the human being as an entity? What is involved here is the anthropologicality of anthropology. At a later stage in this debate, I will pay special attention to the ideas put forward by Lévi-Strauss. In fact, I think that some of his main arguments seem compatible, at least heuristically, with an in-depth study of a theory of the volume. Every time, I will consider new inputs to clarify the characteristics of and issues involved in the anthropology of the human volume.

3.1. Experience and existence

1. Some anthropologists could then object that they are no longer interested in cultures and that these merely represent a pretext to consider actions (as mentioned above) and experiences. They are right. For example, a substantial amount of research, especially in the United States, using a phenomenological or existential anthropology approach[3], is explicitly working on experiences and existences towards a clear empirical goal. What does this have to do with my argument here? Indeed, "culture" as a theoretical framework and structuring entity is often challenged in these anthropological approaches. However, I would like to ask these anthropologists whether lived experiences, interiority, or what concerns the forms of consciousness, and existences are not immediately put into relation in different ways with and within specific social, cultural and political contexts, as if this operation were inherent and necessary in anthropology. Above all, is it not social situations and collective phenomena that represent the ultimate goal for these analyses? How and why do such analyses move away from the human volume himself or do not focus on him? I am not directing a criticism but pointing out an epistemological operation that involves not looking at a human being radically. These kinds of research lose or bypass the human being in several ways, which may add up, not necessarily all according to the authors' approaches. Let us consider in more detail how this happens. The human being may first be lost as a volumic

---

3 A substantial bibliography can be found in [WIL 12].

entity to the advantage of some privileged voluments and specific themes associated in this type of analysis with the notion of experience (by this, I mean the lived experience of something, emotions, affects, modes of consciousness, moral experience, but also bodily and sensory experience, namely a group of voluments that characterize the sphere of interiority and experience). Anthropologists then forget that lived experiences (illness, mourning or migration), in particular feelings and affects, are only some voluments of the anthropological volume, even if they may affect other voluments. This kind of focus, which guides the analysis, makes it possible in a certain way to overlook the volume as such in his entirety and relegate him nearly to the background, to different degrees according to the anthropologists and the type of research in question. As I have pointed out before, we must not forget how relevant it is to consider the continuity and stability of the volume, his stylistic elements and some voluments, which are not affected by a lived experience of any kind. This is one of the issues involved in focusing on the volume, which becomes all the more important as the volume, thus fragmented and reduced as he lives a specific experience, can also be reduced because he is considered in a social position, a role, an activity and a particular state (for example as a religious celebrant, a refugee or someone ill) and because he has been chosen due to one of these characteristics in a situation or a specific framework. Thus, his experience or his existence are "sucked up" and put into perspective in social, cultural, political or economic contexts, alongside their constraints, devices and distinguishing features, which an anthropologist ultimately aims to clarify or attempts to understand in relation to their effect on or, in any case, connection with individuals. Therefore, fragmentation and contextualization complement each other so as to prevent the human being and the volume himself from being the central figure. The volume is thus lost. Sometimes, the methodological tool employed is life stories, together with what they entail almost necessarily: a potential retrospective coherence effect and the exclusion of details and the contingencies of concrete instants – which I think are essential for a basic type of anthropologicality. The same volume may also be diluted in analyses that hinge directly on intersubjectivities or social relations: the volume as he interacts with other humans or with objects or gods in a specific situation or environment prevails over the volumic unity itself. Such angles do not concern the volume himself in his entirety and the nuances of his instants and continuity. Moreover, in these analyses, which focus on some voluments in particular or put the volume into relation, this volume may be gathered and combined in the description with other volumes, precisely to identify a social feature or even to conceive some forms of cultural socialization, for example involving embodiment. The volume observed may also be lost as an entity when a researcher presents as essential his own relations, and his experience of them, with the individual(s) concerned. Evidently, in anthropology this is a classic point, besides being very prominent in the phenomenological or existential anthropology tradition, and in the debates about the ensuing epistemological specificities, whereas the volumological method put forward here relies on a type of withdrawal of the observer from the being observed, as I have pointed out. This method entails looking from a significant distance at human beings as volumes: being astonished at their singularity and movements, and learning thus to observe them and describe them. Finally, as I have mentioned before, there is the potential risk of undermining the human volume in a description similar to a story, a narrative or even a literary exercise that may naturally give a certain depth to some characters but does not necessarily look for a level of precise details, as "raw" as possible in anticipation of comparative analyses. It is as if the volume himself eluded a researcher's writings and narrative goals. Listed as such, these types of interpretation seem to me to mirror the history of social and cultural anthropology, foregrounding intersubjectivities, interactions, language and stories, but also in some cases cultural models. Two collective works, a recent one and an older one [CSO 94, RAM 15], demonstrate how anthropology is considered in relation and reference to a phenomenological or existential tradition. Therefore, various works of this kind – I would include those based on psychological but also cognitive anthropology – often entail an emphasis on parts or aspects (more or less psychological, linked in any case to the sphere of subjectivity and cognition) of individuals related and assembled in sociocultural contexts. Sarah Willen and Don Seeman sum up very clearly, on the basis of a wide variety of ethnographic works, this central point:

> The turn to experience in contemporary anthropology has not, for the most part, involved a collapse of concern for the whole gamut of social and cultural features of human life. Rather, it has more typically provided a conceptual bridge between individual lifeworlds and the much broader political-economic trends and cultural-symbolic systems that constrain and inform them. [WIL 12, p. 6]

Jan Patrick Heiss finds this reluctance to grasp the human entity in itself, for example, in the work of Michael Jackson – who naturally cannot be reduced to or summed up in this element. Heiss points out that the strength of Jackson's existential reading lies more in how different events or various social situations are pertinently interpreted and clarified than in an observation focused on human beings themselves and for themselves [HEI 15a, pp. 259–260]. Human beings are in any case conceived mostly in their relations, which are in this framework regarded as essential for an understanding of human existence[4]. This remark holds true for various types of research associated or not with existential anthropology. This implies another criticism leveled at a specific kind of analysis – once again I am thinking, among others, of Michael Jackson's recent book [JAC 16] – which is characteristic of a type of oscillating thinking and writing, shifting between on polarities. This may be presented as an argument to express experience as well as without fixing it in possible concepts that are too rigid. In my opinion, a line of thinking or a type of writing that claim to waver between general polarities and dichotomies, for example, between the individual and society, subjective and objective, singular and plural, or many others, cannot express the complexity of the volume. This is the case not only because such poles do not necessarily have the same ontological status or do not directly concern the volume himself, but also because, trying to somehow take into consideration through these oscillation levels the experiences encountered and various types of relations entails the risk of being less precise about the entities themselves, who can only be individual and singular. Conceptually, existence needs to be tightened and delimited if the aim is to observe and describe the existent himself. I believe more in the descriptive effectiveness of a cumulative type of writing and line of thinking based on a single pole, that is, the human volume. This involves describing his different voluments, adding and nuancing, with an infinite number of details or specifications which indicate, for example, continuity and lessereity. I think it is relevant to say that if the anthropology of existence (or existants) must exist – and it is important that it does – it will involve a radical emphasis on the volume himself, rigorous methodologies, detailed descriptions[5] and specific concepts, without being necessarily filtered by various philosophies.

2. The human volume is actually not grasped by analyses in terms of experience and existence. Is this very surprising in a context of

---

4 I would like to refer to Laurent Denizeau's analysis [DEN 15].
5 In relation to details, Hans Lucht upholds a different point of view in a chapter of his work *What is Existential Anthropology?* [LUC 15].

phenomenological references? Of course, phenomenology includes a series of various works, interpretations and practices, some of which may undoubtedly be more easily re-appropriable than others to conceive the observation of a human volume. Why then do the anthropologists who belong to the "phenomenologico-existential" tradition encounter difficulties in or are against looking at the human being himself? Do the very foundations of phenomenology not contain in themselves some possible explanations for this bypass? In any case, they constitute a set of thoughts and ideas that can account for it. On a general level, besides the strong focus on particular voluments, experiences, affects, perception, intentions or the body, one cannot underestimate how in several basic phenomenological texts (especially Husserl, Heidegger or Merleau-Ponty's texts), well known in the social sciences, it is possible to see the temptation to present a human being, consciousness and body, both in relation to the world, in it, open to it, ready to be with others, with an intentionality that links him to beings, or even in intercorporal reciprocity. Naturally, these elements are more or less emphasized according to the authors in question, there is no lack of nuances, and differences can become significant between the philosophers but also within a single work. However, the presence of these relational elements allows the social sciences in particular to think that the world, the others, intersubjectivity, community and methodological debates may be regarded as more important than the human entity in phenomenology. Regarding an individual as a volume with his delimited unity and consistency requires in any case a certain amount of alertness to interpretations that favor his relation to what surrounds him or present existence as something that is escaping from itself. On the contrary, the volume is conceived in his consistency, as if separate from the others and the world, and it is this separation that immediately implies permanently, as a structural element of the volume besides relation and intention, a dis-relation and a dis-intention, as is shown by the principle of lessereity and stylistic appropriation[6].

2.1. More specifically, always with regard to the foundations of phenomenology, I will discuss specific critical issues with the three authors cited, not necessarily the same for each author and out of other possible issues, which can shed light on the status or non-status of the human being in whom I am interested. I recall Blumenberg's criticism of Husserl's

---

6 Once again, these remarks of course do not imply that there are no conceptual resources, let alone different observational approaches, in *Being and Time*, *Phenomenology of Perception*, or *Analyses Concerning Passive and Active Synthesis* (by Husserl).

phenomenology and its "anthropological prohibition", which sees "man falling, so to speak, outside of any systematic framework, or if you prefer: he passes through it" [BLU 11, p. 44]. Husserl viewed anthropology as a "philosophical underestimation" and believed that "philosophy and phenomenology can achieve more" [BLU 11, p. 46]. The epistemological aim of phenomenology constitutes then a criticism of scientific types of knowledge, which it censures for their fascination with empirical facts in determined spatiotemporal frameworks. This is what phenomenology wishes to leave behind by asserting the point of view of "essence". As Laurent Perreau writes, "it is just by turning away from the individual that it lays down its project" [PER 08, p. 77]. The eidetic reduction, such as it has been laid as the very foundation of phenomenology, involves conceiving real, concrete and unique individuals as variations based on which, beyond "factual singularity" and the "individual fact", we should look for what is left unchanged and necessary in them, that is, some "essential predicates". This is the very role of *epoché* as a way of "putting into brackets": "It invalidates systematically the individual as individual to enable the prominence of essence" [PER 08, p. 84]. Empirical individuals, those in the here-and-now, are in reality regarded as illustrations, examples and actual variations, among other variations, of "essence", which is a kind of *a priori* structure. Husserl aimed to purify his examples, removing the various contingencies and vague or indistinct elements [VER 99]. On the contrary, these are details and nuances that an anthropologist looks for, when focused on the empirical entirety of the volume, and simultaneously on the nuances of the voluments. I should mention another point: the acts and experiences of consciousness elude these reductions and exclusions of the individual or the empirical world. The issue involves consciousness of the correlation between the subject and the world, and consciousness as constitution and unification of the beings and objects. *Epoché* implies getting rid of an object in order to bring out more clearly the acts of consciousness, with their various expressions[7], and describing them. From these phenomenological operations, it is indeed the dependence of beings and things on a subjectivity and on the activities of an intentional consciousness that is emphasized. Thus, Husserl wrote that "no thing has its individuality in itself" [HUS 80, p. 313]. Given that things are not individualized in themselves, "they appear as such only and always to a consciousness [...]. Ultimately, it is the act of consciousness that establishes the spatiotemporal position of existence" [PER 08, p. 87]. In these perspectives, concrete individuals are left behind to

---

7 I am thinking, for example, about the modes of attention: see [HUS 09] and [DEP 14].

discover essences, and they are regarded as without having an existence in itself but as relative to consciousnesses and subjectivities. In short, from such phenomenological analyses, we can first identify all the importance given to subjective life and to the acts and experiences of consciousness, as if they occupied an almost absolute space in the volumes of being and were an integral part of them. We can also note in these analyses the emphasis on the subjectivity and experience of a researcher during his work, so that this experience may become the research topic instead of the observed volume. On the contrary, volumography focuses on bringing into relief the human volume and each specific volume as separate from his context – even if he is still loosely related to it – without turning the context into the focus or letting it suck up human beings. The empirical volume is observed through the distance allowed by methods and concepts, so that he appears to an observer in his consistency and yet remains independent of his view, while his acts of consciousness are only some voluments among other voluments[8].

2.2. It is also necessary to recall that Heidegger, in a different philosophical theory, regards anthropology as "a kind of dumping ground" [HEI 62, p. 269], adding that philosophical anthropology is characterized by "its indefinites and its intrinsic limitations" [HEI 62, p. 220] and that it is in dire need of explanation and ontological foundations. To this end, according to Heidegger's goal itself, "existential analytic", which searches for *a priori* structures, "is prior to any psychology, anthropology, and especially biology" [HEI 10, p. 44]. Blumemberg mentions Heidegger's "phobia" of anthropology [BLU 11, p. 103]. The doubt about sciences, which he criticizes like Husserl, the lack of interest in the concrete manifestations of an individual, and the disregard for the empirical as well as for the human are typical of Heidegger's ideas and combine with one another. In *Discourse on Thinking*, Heidegger wrote:

> Scientist: Even so, it is a mystery to me how man's nature is ever to be found by looking away from man.

---

8 A few years ago, I put forward the term "phenomenography" to indicate the detailed observation–description of humans, one at a time, as I have pointed out above, including observable actions or gestures and feelings in their succession of singular moments with the aim of circumventing some phenomenological principles as well as their ethnographic emphasis on relations and groups. See [KNE 19] for more information on this topic and in debates with phenomenology.

> Teacher: It is a mystery to me too; so I seek to clarify how far
> this is possible, or perhaps even necessary. [HEI 66, p. 58]

This seems very important to me. Just as if anthropology did not stop haunting fundamental ontology [ROM 10, p. 464], the fact is that the "being-in-the-world" is at the center of *Being and Time* and "existential analytic". Heidegger characterizes him as he who dwells in, inhabits, and is in relation with the world, interacting with its beings and things [HEI 86, p. 88 and ff.]. Thus, this being has become a "being-with" in a "with-world" [HEI 10, p. 116]. That was enough for the social sciences in general and some anthropologists to become empirically interested in the being-in-the-world, who became a central theme in their phenomenological and existential approaches. Yet, they adopt this theme with their own perspective or line of thinking, since in most cases what is empirically recalled from the "being-in-the-world", independently of the reference itself to Heidegger, is the "in" with its variants (with, within) or the "world" with its interrelated components. The human entity, as I have already pointed out, is somehow sucked up and the observer's view focuses, on the one hand, on the way in which the being is sucked up in the world, observed and conceived "as" in relation to other humans, organisms or objects, in his links to, his attachment to, his immersion in, his actions in, and his relations to, and, on the other hand, on the world itself, the situation, the space, the environment, or the others, or on a specific social phenomenon. The being-in-the-world is thus not extracted from the world, but quite the opposite[9]. I think that the expression "being-in-the-world" excessively favors relationist types of focus. It sums up a significant part of the approaches adopted in the social sciences in various forms and to different degrees: relational being, being with, being situated, immersed, etc. Looking at a volume implies not attaching importance too quickly to the world, because the volume, given that he is a volume, turns away from the world just as he is part of it. It is interesting to note that Heidegger, while explaining the *Dasein*, does not fail to focus on a being who is, regardless of his actions, "in subservience" to or under the "domination" of public life [HEI 10, pp. 122–123]. He is "completely taken in by the world and the Dasein-with of the others" [HEI 10, p. 169]. This causes him to wander from and let go of himself, as Heidegger remarks. Specifically, "the others have taken its being away from it" [HEI 10, p. 122][10]. Thus, this being is distanced from himself, in his "mode

---

9 About this point of view, see, for instance, the recent paper of Jason Throop [THR 18].
10 According to Heidegger's words applied to the *Dasein*.

of average everydayness" [HEI 10, p. 43], which unburdens him of his singularity and authenticity. According to Heidegger, this represents his escape from himself [HEI 10, p. 122 and ff.][11]. However, according to the theory of the volume, a volume does not turn away from himself, since he constantly and ineluctably returns to himself and is always held back. What he turns away from are mostly relations, the others and the actions carried out with them. Literally, through his unitary way of working, in particular through his style and his withdrawing and regulating lessereity – even when it lessens in one way or another the perceived intensity of his being – the volumic unity remains itself and cannot escape from itself or avoid being itself, as it has been pointed out. The volume cannot avoid appropriating himself and does not have the possibility of choosing himself or losing himself, regardless of his actions, feelings and thoughts (his own or those of others), which are, retained, appropriated and lessened. What the volume indicates is less a unity "ahead of itself" and "beyond itself", worried or preoccupied, according to Heidegger's words [HEI 10, p. 185] – an interpretation that runs the risk of shifting the focus from the volume to his actions – than a restrained being, retained within himself, as it can be seen if the volumic entity is considered seriously and thoroughly in his anthropological consistency. Is the aforementioned dis-link from the others actually a refusal, if implicit? It is Merleau-Ponty who suggests this clarification. He writes that "the refusal to communicate, however, is still a form of communication" [MER 45, p. 420]. According to him, the social world is a "permanent field" [MER 45, p. 421] in which every individual is situated and involved. Everyone is "attached" to the world, so that no one can stop being situated in relation to it even if he refuses it or turns away from it: "I may well turns away from it, but not cease to be situated relatively to it" [MER 45, p. 421]. However, it seems to me that the volumic unity does not express first the refusal of a "freedom". In reality, the lessereity principle reveals above all a form of diffuse resistance, expressing the volumic difficulty of being in this common world. It is the sign of a unity that cannot avoid being in it, knowing that it does not manage to be in it because it is such a unity.

2.3. In relation to Merleau-Ponty, I want to highlight only a specific element in the debate in question, about the place occupied by the human entity. Merleau-Ponty significantly stresses his encounter with the ambiguity

---

11 My book on Heidegger [PIE 14b] partially focuses on this element of detachment and unburdening, which is clearly present in his work.

of the human being, who cannot be truly understood according to his various types of conditioning or physiological and psychological features, or his reflective capacity, which allows him to think of himself as the foundations for his actions. When dealing with, for instance, the analysis of the relations between body and mind, faced with, on one hand, sciences which explain and enclose, and on the other hand the emphasis on consciousness, irreducible and in excess, Merleau-Ponty presents the human being as a problem that forces experts, also in the social sciences, to be attentive and self-criticize their research on a permanent basis[12]. "So there cannot in all good conscience be any question of solving the human problem; there can only be a question of describing man as problematic" [MER 64, p. 202]. Concretely, this becomes complex. In fact, according to expressions that are typical of Merleau-Ponty, the individual is naturally not conceived as a "real unity", but he is always "indivisibly demolished and remade by the course of time" [MER 05, p. 255] and the body "is not where it is, nor what it is" [MER 05, p. 229], and even when it allows existence to evade the world, "the body never quite falls back on to itself" [MER 05, p. 191]. The human being in question is in fact "suspended and put on hold in favor of a problematizing type of questions", according to the illuminating remarks made by Étienne Bimbenet on the topic [BIM 01, p. 252]. This becomes "an idea of an inquiry without discovery, a hunt without a kill" [MER 64, p. 202], which naturally makes it possible to question, for example, the body, perception or intersubjectivity, but about a being who does not cease to escape, slide away and slip away. The human being is not regarded as an observable given, as I suggest, but as an event or an advent: "Mind and man never are, they show through in the movement by which the body becomes gesture, language an oeuvre, and coexistence truth" [MER 64, p. 240]. This line of thinking runs the risk of bringing about the predicted end, according to Foucault, of the knowledge of man, which in my opinion has not truly begun. At the very end of *The Order of Things*, Foucault famously points out, that man, a "recent invention" [FOU 05, p. 422], has only posed a problem for knowledge in the last century and a half. He adds that he is already about to fade. He also points out, concerning the human sciences, "not only are they able to do without the, concept of man, they are also unable to pass through it, for they always address themselves to that which constitutes his outer limits" [FOU 05, p. 413]. My proposal attempts to put forward an empirical solution and an approach against a theory of this kind. In any case, the idea of the problematic human that encourages a

---

12 For this debate, see [BIM 01].

problematizing knowledge runs the risk of confirming Blanchot's claim, according to which the absence of man is his only possibility of being present in the humanities: "Man is absent from the human sciences. This does not mean that he is elided or suppressed. On the contrary, it is his only way of being present in them" [BLA 93, p. 250]. I could say that this absence is confirmed in the final ontological remarks made by Merleau-Ponty. There, he spells out that flesh is a "prototype for being" that underlies the mutual insertion and meshwork of "this visible body, and all the visibles with it" [MER 68, p. 138]. He also presents the human being as a "variant" of this "carnal being" (p. 136) and as the element that allows the "visible" to take shape. What an anthropologist needs is a "hunt" with a "kill" – if one uses the words of Merleau-Ponty, precisely the human volume, who is a distinctly present given. In which aspect indeed is this ambiguity of the human being so problematic, both for him and for the observer? Does this analysis not involve some exaggerations? Does the epistemological debate not run the risk of being overstated with an emphasis on the "problematic" dimension of the human being? One of the goals of the volume is to provide a "grip" and make it possible, as his various compresent voluments combine and dis-combine in the volume himself, to relieve the human entity of different metaphysical and epistemological burdens, which turn him into an "object" that is impossible or, more precisely, problematic. I think it is important for an anthropologist not to bear the burden of all these difficulties, otherwise his object may be constantly bypassed, without, however, de-characterizing the human being in any way. In short, on the one hand, each human being is too unique, concrete or problematic in the epistemological debates of phenomenology while, on the other hand, the social sciences do not hesitate to extend the emphasis on the relational expressions of human beings. The human being as an empirical entity is lost in both cases. I think that some anthropological approaches, inspired in several ways by phenomenology – it should be pointed out that phenomenology cannot be reduced to the three philosophies mentioned – and despite the empirical goal of anthropologists associated with ethnographic investigations, may keep track of such lines of thought, even if these are not necessarily made explicit. At least, they may potentially relegate the human being, the individual himself, and his singularity to a secondary position, and in a way exempt a researcher from questioning this point. Some traces of phenomenological discourses may also be identified in the focus especially on the modalities and expressions of consciousness and lived experience, in the questionable level of detail of the descriptions of human modes of presence – as if it were not the human being who comes first – and in the debates about the epistemological uncertainties and difficulties encountered in phenomenological or existential ethnography[13]. Rather than "essences", it is also situations, worlds and contexts that re-establish themselves (they had also been put on hold by Husserl's *epoché*) as counterweights to the potential idealistic tendency of phenomenology and in order to guarantee the empirical validity of the descriptions. But in doing so, the contexts are used to turn away from the human being. In these ethnographic approaches, consciousnesses, relations and contexts indeed come first, and the human being remains in the background, whereas the volumographic approach foregrounds him[14].

3.2. Going beyond, wrenching and eccentricity

1. We do not leave experience and existence. For the latter in particular, the topic or the concept, Sartre's ideas constitute a theoretical framework that is favored in existential anthropology[15]. It is only from this perspective and in the search for explanations of the status set for the human being that I frame the debate. Therefore, in the aforementioned Sartrean discourse, it is necessary to identify several points that, in my opinion, constitute an issue for existential anthropology and its ways of keeping the focus on the human being, and also when its goal is to conceive, according to social situations, the human condition. I can only endorse Sartre's request to study "that privileged existant which is man (privileged for us)" [SAR 63, p. 168] and his critique of the "sciences of man", which "do not question man" but "the development and the relation of human facts" (p. 168). Nevertheless, as I have already pointed out, faced with the volumic reality to be described, it is difficult to accept a definition of existence as a "project" and "by going beyond of a situation" (p. 91) or of the human being "by what he succeeds in making of what he has been made" (p. 91). Quite explicitly, actions and relations remain clearly at the center and the requirement for details as

---

13 Among other points, the issue may also concern the opacity of beings, the limitations of methods and concepts, or the role of the ethnographer involved. An article mentioned above [WIL 12] is instructive in this respect.

14 I will thus be skeptical about the possibility for a "new humanism" in anthropology based on the phenomenologico-existential approaches, since, as I have attempted to show, anthropology has never really been "human-centered", but also since many such approaches circumvent again the human being. See the very insightful paper by [WEN 18].

15 This can be seen, for example, in some parts of [JAC 15].

"differentials", which Sartre recommends in order to seize singularity (p. 137), is not easily fulfilled in such an approach. Undoubtedly, what is unique and individual singularity are no longer disregarded. However, it should not come as a surprise that, in her comments on Sartre, Iris Murdoch notes indeed that he highlights the study of a particular case but that, when he presents it as a "totality" and structures it around the individual's choice, his freedom, or the way in which he goes beyond situation behind, Sartre neglects the diversity of details and ultimately describes, as Murdoch writes, a consciousness that is too transparent, too abstracted and in the end too distant from the imperfections of each individual's relations [MUR 53]. In addition, as it emphasizes continuity, the anthropology of volumes is nearly the opposite of Sartre's goal in his biographies and autobiographies, which involve, according to Philippe Lejeune's comments [LEJ 89, p. 100 and ff.]: not respecting the chronological order which would imply a restricted way of conceiving time, conceiving the human being as a type of "freedom" which, in a situation, "invents a way out of it" [LEJ 89, p. 103], and identifying the "project" of the individual "perceived as the sole direction of the individual's most characteristic ways of behaving" [LEJ 89, p. 103] and studied as a central element in his life, alongside a reading hypothesis that pushes the chronology of actions and events to the background. This is the line of thinking adopted by Sartre in his analysis of Flaubert: "we feel obscurely that Flaubert had not 'received' his ambition [...] Neither heredity, nor bourgeois background nor education can account for it". Sartre puts these various explanations aside and regards Flaubert's goal as "a fact with all a fact's contingency" [SAR 56, p. 560]. This point of view lacks all the consistency of the volume and the voluments he contains, at each moment and as time goes by. It is not an accurate representation of the concrete continuity of a volume. This is the empirical and methodological difficulty encountered in descriptions based on continuity and avoided by Sartre's discourse, which emphasizes the totality of an "impulse towards being" [SAR 56, p. 563]. It is exactly this type of interpretation that makes it even more necessary to describe the human being in precise terms. Sartre uses a far too voluntarist vocabulary, which may shed light on stories but not on reality. In stories, events, behaviors and feelings are not organized chronologically, as Lejeune explains, but as "signs to be deciphered, in order to reconstitute a project" [LEJ 89, p. 103]. In the concrete reality, there is a chronological sequence that must be reconstructed. Therefore, the aim of volumuography – let's use this term to refer to observations made over a given period of time – is not to create a concise biographical account based on events that may seem to stand out. Instead, its goal is to find the real continuity of instants. This continuity contains observable and explanatory elements. It is a succession of moments, situations, sequences, small volumuations, small variations, acts and words, which leave some traces – small or big, accumulated, immediate, or distant – but also lessening appropriations and the continuity of stylistic forms, all within the consistency of the volume. This way of observing voluments and the continuous reality hardly validates Sartre's view, which presents a human being in a "particular empirical situation", through "the production of himself in the world" [SAR 63, p. 147] and a "personalization" process, like "a way of going beyond" [SAR 87]. Is there really a "going beyond" or an invention? Is it possible to observe a "going beyond" and an invention? In relation to what? As I have pointed out, there is an interplay of contingencies and a variety of compresences among voluments according to the moment, and there are also voluments that may elude social marks. However, is what may resemble a "going beyond" these social marks not rooted in the very style of a volume and in what he contains? I think so. Could a gradual change in stylistic traits concern some voluments? However, this implies that style itself, associated with other voluments of the volume, such as types of knowledge and know-hows, can do so. In any case, I think that "going beyond" or "invention" are words that typically refer to what is carried and pervaded by the stylistic voluments of the volume, whose genealogy and development can be observed moment after moment. Ultimately, it is not surprising that the theory of the volume, which emphasizes the continuity and stability of the volumic entity, is at odds with a classic theme in existentialist philosophy, that is, the idea of wrenching, such as Sartre himself mentions it: "This is what we call existence, and by this we do not mean a stable substance which rests in itself, but rather a perpetual disequilibrium, a wrenching away from itself with all its body" [SAR 63, p. 151]. This idea put forward by Sartre may seem strange to an observer who wants to look closely. It typically reveals the importance of the notion of volume: tightening the notion of existence as one of the conditions that must be met to seize it and observe it, as I have already pointed out. The volume observed is, indeed, a continuous unity who goes on by never ceasing to return to himself, while acting, marking his acts, and appropriating external things. Therefore, when conceived as intrinsically volumic or volumized, existence seems least of all a wrenching away. Let us say that a volume is, through his stability and ability to retain or hold back his acts, a type of insistence, even when he attempts to express or do something, and feels an imbalance. Would it then be better to refer to insistential volumology? As an ideal goal, the empirical continuism of the anthropology of concrete volumes seems to me in any case an answer to the questions about determinacies and freedoms. Often, we prefer to leave the questions open and not find the answers contained in empirical reality.

1.1. The human being as he is wrenched away, ahead of and beyond himself, is a classic topic in existentialism and phenomenology. This theme can be found in the recent discussion of Étienne Bimbenet in relation to another theoretical proposal. Here, the human being is presented in his relation to a set of "common fictions", for example language, culture or rules, with the aim – and this is a crucial point – of conceiving an anthropological difference and criticizing "zoocentrism" as the attitude of an age that does not want to consider the human being and "what is specifically human" [BIM 17, p. 24]. This goal is all the more interesting for my remarks. Naturally, I fully subscribe to the strong criticism leveled at this prevailing zoocentrism. However, I cannot see in the author's suggestions an alternative way of laying the foundations for an observation of the human being. Not only does the demand to study "life as it is subjectively lived" [BIM 17, p. 33], which underlies that work, focus on some voluments (i.e. feelings, affects, consciousness) of the volume but, above all, conceiving man as wrenched away is undoubtedly a way of bypassing the human being. He is not wrenched away, he does not elude himself, and he cannot avoid being himself. Thus, one of his distinguishing features is to be a unity that is held back and retained, as I have pointed out. The human being is described at length in the book of Étienne Bimbenet as he is about to "be wrenched away" to play "the game of social rules" [BIM 17, p. 206] or on the verge of "freeing himself from himself enough" [BIM 17, p. 250] to live in a shared world. I could add many more citations like these that involve the idea of wrenching away, which is quite different from the volume folding back on and resting on himself such as I conceive him. Eluding or wrenching away implies a gap and a break. Voluments, types of knowledge, know-hows, abilities and style cannot avoid themselves, their "content" and their "expression". If a volume may seem to be going beyond himself· or wrenching himself away from himself, it is according to his own capacities or modes of being and the voluments that hold him back and retain him. Therefore, there is no wrenching away or going beyond. Human volumes can only pretend to wrench themselves away. I think that humankind, which was regarded as secondary when it was absorbed into the supernatural sphere or animality, as E. Bimbenet claims, comes always second when it is associated with a "disentanglement" from oneself and a "displacement" in culture, language or institutions, and when it is shown to contain "a living being wrenched away from himself with the aim of a truth that applies to all" [BIM 17, p. 263]. The success of the animal as a topic in anthropology diverts attention away from the human being, fundamentally in keeping with the traditional epistemology of anthropology. However, subjectivity considered as he wrenches away from himself and the dimension into which he projects himself represent another way of turning away from the volume, that is, this human who, in reality, only attempts to achieve something and who expresses something without going out of himself and wrenching himself away from himself, always held back, as I have pointed out in these pages. In fact, how can I seize a human being who is about to be wrenched away from himself, and first how can I think that he can in this condition be observed in his details? Considering the human being as he wrenches himself away from himself implies not looking at him. Naturally, it may be acknowledged that these regulated and instituted worlds create some of the distinguishing features of human life – arguing, convincing, passing on, and referring to laws and traditions. But in doing so, these worlds have relegated the human being to the background and become the very basis of the thematic shift in the humanities and the social sciences: "Language and rules drive us as living beings far from ourselves" [BIM 17, p. 271]. It is as if, in the end, the human being were less important than "truth, good, or beauty" [BIM 17, p. 35]. As a subjective volume who projects himself relationally and a wrenched volume, as if losing himself to the advantage of the common worlds, the human being is hard to look at. It is not because he is a volume that he can wrench himself away from himself. He cannot wrench himself away because he is a volume held together. All these remarks lead to these points: considering first and foremost the subjectivity of the volume implies highlighting one volument among others; conceiving the human being as he wrenches himself away from himself towards other realities implies forgetting the volumic density, which continues moment after moment, is always nuanced, and combines and marks voluments, as it attempts to use minimally various cultural realities, relying on them and turning away from them according to a characteristic lessereity. It also provides the possibility of diverting attention to the cultural productions in question, which have been stabilized and are situated outside the volume, for example, language and various institutions. It is then some traces left by the human being that are considered, but the volume himself is bypassed. In any case, the human entity as central figure is lost. Philosophical debates make it also easier to understand the difficulty involved in keeping the human being in his volumic radicality.

1.2. In another order of ideas, that is, German philosophical anthropology, Plessner's line of thinking is sometimes in line with Étienne Bimbenet's when it tends to conceive the volume as he devolumizes himself. At first sight, these ideas of Helmuth Plessner may seem close my topic. It is important to emphasize the fact that the human volume necessarily occupies his own position in space and not someone else's position, and that he cannot get rid of the limitations of his physical body which, while also allowing him to open up to others, fences in him too. This is what Plessner names "positionality", which characterizes a state of "being posed" [PLE 17, p. 238]. It is "in no way a construction, but an acquisition made directly in relation to the visible structure" [PLE 17, p. 59][16]. I want to emphasize that this limit is inherent in the body. It is "the mark of the outlines" with its "identifiable limits" [PLE 17, p. 247]. However, I think that it is first the limit of the volume instead of a boundary that he "accomplishes" [PLE 17, p. 204] and has the possibility of "going beyond" [PLE 17, p. 242], as Plessner also notes when he conceives the boundary separating the organism and his environment as "fluctuating" and always to be concretized or invented [SOM 13, p. 55]. There is another point that Plessner uses to develop his own representation of the human being, that is, "eccentric positionality" that implies a reflexive overhang and his "objectivation" in cultural artificiality [PLE 17, p. 441 and ff.]. In order to point out such capacities, Plessner emphasizes in turn a kind of escape of the human being from himself [SOM 13]. Plessner writes that "man remains outside himself" [PLE 17, p. 455], as in a state of imbalance. Once again, this vocabulary is especially striking and in conflict with the "holding-retaining" element that the human volume, when properly considered, encourages us to understand. The more I look at human beings as volumes, the less I think that their position is eccentric. I will ask this question once again: eccentric in relation to what? As for the way in which they go on, volumes are not "outside" themselves, but they always return to and face themselves, keeping a kind of center of gravity in themselves. This may seem evident, and it certainly is for Plessner, even though his vocabulary does not fail to emphasize this "being-outside-oneself" [PLE 17, p. 448] and "beyond oneself" [PLA 17, p. 236]. It

---

16 Given that this work by Plessner has not been translated into English yet as this book is put to press, these passages are noted according to the French translation.

may be words or utterances and his various productions or cultural fabrications that lie outside or beyond the volume and that he lets slide away. However, it is not the being or the volume himself who eludes himself – on the contrary, he is held back in himself – nor is it his thoughts, even reflexive or fleeting, or actions, which indeed attempt to express and manifest themselves, but without any escape from the volume since, on the contrary, they are characterized by him and some of his voluments. In relation to the volume's acts, which are always about to be held back by him and some voluments, as I have pointed out, the "ec-" of eccentricity (or the "ex" of existence) cannot refer to any escape. Once again, the volume is a structure held and retained rather than escaping. If a volume can feel some imbalance, these feelings are his own and constitute his own voluments. Plessner reproaches Husserl for prioritizing consciousness and subjectivity, as he prefers to conceive the phenomenality of the living world [GUI 17, p. 8], as the presentation of *The Levels of the Organic Life* explains. What I find awkward is considering the human being eccentrically: I think that in doing so, the volumic mode of the human being cannot be expressed with precision and observed properly.

2. These remarks and the previous ones confirm that the anthropology of volumes can be identified more clearly and without any ambiguity if it is presented as an exist*a*ntial anthropology[17], which is radically focused on empirical existents in their continuity of instants and complemented by a search for their modalities of structuration. This makes it possible to mark my shift in focus: existence is no longer conceived as action, relation or going beyond, but the existent himself is conceived as a volume. This makes it also possible to avoid any potential confusion, in particular, in relation to existentialist approaches. Volumology corresponds to a radical existantism, which I also prefer to spell with an "a" – to confirm the aforementioned clarification. Therefore, I hope it will be clear that it is possible, and even essential, to implement an existantial type of anthropology, without any reference to Heidegger, Sartre or any other philosophy, but also without working on so-called existential themes (time, pain, death, critical situations, moments or events). It is in these terms that I conceive this type of existantial anthropology as the goal of anthropology, so that it can free itself from its social and cultural tradition resting on social phenomena, cultural systems, actions and relations, situations, or events, and reach its goal: the human being.

---

17 See the remark about this spelling in the preface of this book.

3.3. Lines and flow

1. In connection with phenomenology and also the notion of being-in-the-world, Tim Ingold's inquiries see "human life" as the ultimate goal of anthropology, and yet they push the dilution of the human entity to its extreme based on strong relationist foundations. The phenomenological option is complemented by the influence of Deleuze's philosophy as well as the reference to ecology and its vocabulary, which is often presented as the science of the relations among organisms and between organisms and the world that surrounds them. In this sense, Ingold notes, for example, that "the organism-in-its-environment *is* a being-in-the-world" [ING 18, p. 95][18]. I will only mention a few elements of Ingold's huge oeuvre. I am immediately questioned by his presentation of living beings as "lines", which combine with one another to form the meshwork of social life. Ingold writes that "every living being is a line or, better, a bundle of lines" [ING 16, p. 10]. Therefore, he sees social life as an "interpenetration" of lines, which he indeed regards as different from a collective fusion. This lexical choice naturally depends on a relational type of ontology. Ingold, referring to Mauss, writes that "through the gift, my awareness penetrates yours – I am *with* you in your thoughts – and in your counter-gift, you are *with* me in mine. And so long as we continue to give and receive, this interpenetration can perdure" [ING 16, p. 10]. These are his comments on interpenetrating relations:

> Relations are ways living beings have of going along together, and – as they do – of forging each other's existence [...]. Beings-in-relation are "mutually constituted". To put it more simply, your relations with others get inside you and make you the being you are. And they get inside the others as well. [ING 18, pp. 102–103]

It is in this context that choosing lines as a metaphor is useful to describe movements of this kind: "the entwined lines of the meshwork join with one another, and, in so doing, possess an inner feel for each other and are not simply linked by external contiguity" [ING 16, p. 12]. Thus, from this perspective, beings conceived as lines are joined, tangled and interlaced, "responding" and "transforming" one another in a "perpetual renewal"

---

18 I would like to thank Tim Ingold for allowing me to read the drafts of this book before its actual publication.

[ING 16, p. 16]. What Ingold describes in these terms is more easily accomplished by malleable lines than by volumes with their consistency, who resist what happens, advance but are always held back before the others, and hardly ever change, such as I have described them. When it comes to volumes, the idea of interpenetration does not seem the most relevant for a description of the movement of the aforementioned rays. Human beings are not lines, even if body tissues with their various threads, known by the anatomists mentioned by Ingold, may call them to mind [ING 11, pp. 86–87]. In reality, human beings are volumes. One could object to me that intertwined lines may constitute a volume. However, a volume is indeed a volume before constituting every time a new tangle of lines. Even if we have seen the variety of compresences in a volume, several stabilized voluments cannot become interwoven and intertwined as flexibly as lines. Besides, it is for this reason that I preferred referring to compresence to define the way in which they combine and structure themselves. In Ingold's theory, lines have various relational capacities – this may even be their main feature – and could not be conceived as parts of the volume, which they would depend on. I see these lines as a flattening of the volume and the volumic density. Typically, it is density, and therefore the precise composition of voluments, that is questioned and, in a way, suspended. Ingold also points out that these lines are not an interaction or an intersubjectivity of points situated opposite one another. These lines go along and are joined with other lines. Seen as such, beings are then described as uninterruptedly modified, doing more than being, as Ingold says, involved in action, practical commitment, their attentive feeling, with each of the others, and immersed in their environment [ING 11, p. 10], like an octopus in his environment [ING 17, p. 18]. For example, Ingold points out that distraction is merely attention diverted in a different direction [ING 16, p. 19], as if avoiding this immersion were impossible[19]. Undoubtedly, much more could be said about Ingold's lines. I would like to add another point to this critique of devolumizing lines. I find here a more radical position, which is somehow diametrically opposed to the volumist approach and implies in fact a dilution of beings with an effect that is nearly avolumizing. Thus, it seems that Ingold is not looking for "delimited entities" but "nexuses composed of knotted lines whose loose ends spread in all directions, tangling with other lines in other knots" [ING 13b, p. 9], in a "continual interchange of materials across ever-growing and ever-shedding layers of skin" [ING 13b,

19 As I have noted above, I see distraction more as an attenuated form of attention and a way of not pushing it to its extreme in a given direction.

p. 10]. The environment is not what surrounds us but a "zone of interpenetration in which our own and others' lives are comprehensively entangled" [ING 13a, p. 10]. There are no humans on one side and an external environment on the other, but an "indivisible totality" [ING 00, p. 19], "a field of relations which, as it unfolds, actively and ceaselessly brings forms into being" [ING 00, p. 51]. Naturally, there are differences between forms, but in a reading of this kind I am not looking for singular individuals who should be observed and described in and of themselves. In fact, no entity can be isolated. Each has its place only as process and movement, "generated within a relational field that cuts across the interface within its environment" [ING 90, p. 220]. According to Ingold, the "loose pieces can only be used to think about machines but not life. If life is to be found again, it is important to conceive it not as a separate entity but as "the unfolding of a continuous and ever-evolving field of relations" [ING 11, p. 237], specifically, biological and social relations among humans and between humans and other species. It is certainly not because he is a well-delimited entity that a living being can be conceived as a meshwork of lines, but because of his permeability, which enables flows, mixtures and transformations, or at most fleeting solidifications, in a "relational matrix within which forms, both human and non-human, are generated and sustained" [ING 18, p. 104]. Therefore, this entails that humans and other living beings, immersed and interpenetrated, can be presented as somewhat equivalent. Incontestably, Ingold wants to give a specific focus to anthropology, especially to understand "biosocial becomings". He is right when he distinguishes it from its sociological and culturalist tradition, which, on the contrary, the ontological turn pushes to its extreme. However, the fact remains that in Ingold's ideas the human volume becomes secondary and is relegated to the background by interpenetrations and environments. Could it be that these aspects manage to dilute the human volume even more than, or at least as much as, social or cultural frameworks? On the one hand, readings of this kind – I am thinking about the quote above on the interpenetration of relations [ING 16, p. 10] – fail to consider the modes of intravolumic appropriation of the voluments of other volumes and present a conceptual approach (e.g. "line" or "interpenetration"), which does not aim to teach to observe and describe human beings or a human being, to delimit him, outline him and look at him. But especially, on the other hand, the very basis for Ingold's relationism excludes this type of view: "In the world of fluid space there are no objects of perception" [ING 11, p. 88]. More directly, resorting to the biological paradigm that studies life as a "continual flow of materials"

[ING 11, p. 86], rather than in delimited forms [ING 2013, p. 195], warrants a lack of focus on the human volume. The principle underlying the theory of the volume is precisely to pay heed to the fact that everyone is and remains a volume of being and well "delimited", regardless of his partial dependence on other beings and what he integrates from the things present in the environment. I would say that the volume comes first; this is a necessary requirement if the goal is to start looking at and describe a human being. Let us recall that it has been defined as the principle of anthropologicality and as the very foundation for anthropology as a field of study. All these elements encourage me also to reconsider the question of the scale of anthropology, which is constantly weakened by sociocultural frameworks or an approach to the human being understood in his environment, but also by the potential shifts towards his biological components and variations, provided that they are rigorously defined – which is not always the case. There is a question that runs through this book and seems greatly needed at this stage: is it not an intrinsic feature of anthropology to put on hold any relational ontology that leads it towards sociology, culturology, ethnology (also called social or cultural anthropology) or ecology in order to become a science of human beings? I will also point out that theoretical stances can be coherently applied to the methodological dimension. As Ingold writes: "Anthropology, in my definition, is *philosophy with the people in*" [ING 18, p. 4]. He also adds his own relational principles: "to observe with is not to objectify; it is to attend to persons and things, to learn from them, and to follow in precept and practice" [ING 16, p. 24]. Thus, Ingold favors an observation "with", whereas I deem it important to "objectify" in order to give rise to an anthropological science not through the classic ethnographic method, which is itself very relational, but through observations focused on humans and precise analyses. Ingold sums up his remarks as follows: "To perceive the environment is not to look back on the things to be found in it, or to discern their congealed shapes and layouts, but to join with them in the material flows and movements contributing to their – and our – ongoing formation" [ING 11, p. 88]. Volumography is indeed opposed to an approach of this kind.

2. These last methodological points refer to what I regard as the key method for the anthropology of human volumes: the "following" of a single volume at a time. This is less a type of following strictly speaking than a continuous focus, an uninterrupted way of looking at a volume as he is living. The words "to follow" or "following", which are often employed to

refer to observations of a being, are quite significant. They may lead us to think that it is not human beings who are the first and ultimate object we should understand. Indeed, this following concerns more movement, activities and actions than the human being himself. In order to establish a volumography, I think it is important to note that the issue is for the observer to be situated before the volume and face him, and therefore to move back when he advances, unless one remains besides him, if this is enough to observe him properly and film him in his actions. The issue is not to be with the volume either, as essentially the whole of ethnography recommends. Therefore, these remarks may lead to some points of Deleuze's philosophy. I do not think that this type of continuous "observation of" focus on a human being corresponds to what Deleuze and Guattari mean by "ambulant sciences", which do not involve reproducing or looking for a form, matter or material, but involve avoiding "the permanence of a fixed point of *view* that is external", following, and being "carried away by a vortical flow" rather than "watching the flow from the bank" [DEL 05, p. 372]. Thus, it is certainly not surprising that Casper Bruun Jensen [CAS 12], when he regards the ethnographer as an example of an "ambulant scientist" according to Deleuze and Guattari's terminology [DEL 05, p. 372], mentions the following of actors, but a type of following which aims to understand practices, concepts, multiple realities and local ontologies, without ever indicating the possibility of following uninterruptedly the reality of the human being himself, which on the contrary aims to understand what a human volume is. In this case, with this goal, I think that detached observation is more adequate than a type of following, thus characterized by an eddying movement. I do not believe it is possible to seize – I use this term on purpose – the substantial presence of a volume with his continuity and aim to observe and describe him if he is immediately conceived as a "flux" – defined in the dictionary as a "flow" – or a movement, a becoming, a trajectory and a line[20]. As has already been said about Ingold's work, the choice of metaphors is not inconsequential. The volumic existence, with its continuing density, cannot be reasonably described and understood if it is associated with lines of any kind. Its continuity is a concrete consistency with what that means, it is not the continuity of a flux. And if there must be a flux, like that of thoughts, often characterized in these terms, it is only an

---

20 The reader may find this terminology in particular in the chapter "Treatise on Nomadology", which is now quite well known in the social sciences and anthropology.

element of the volume of being, who remains this solid unity[21]. Therefore, the anthropological volume is not Deleuze and Guattari's "body without organs". This body, which does not constitute the entire human being, is thought to be made up of "dynamic tendencies involving energy transformation" and conceived as a "connection of desires", "articulation", opening to "connections" and opposition to the "organism", the "organization" and the various layers that "bind" [DEL 05, pp. 149–166]. The volume also does not contain the organs studied by biologists or chemists, but he is the opposite of disarticulation and characterized by a holding and a stability that nothing or nearly nothing can elude, including even those aspects that might seem to disarticulate themselves from him, including desires, intensities or the various forms of "frenzy", held back and retained by the volume and some of his voluments. Their multiplicity, regardless of their kind, is always already contained, retained, appropriated and lessened, as they are unfolding. It could also be noted that "consistency" is a word that can be found in Deleuze's terminology. However, it is something that "knows nothing of substance and form", gathers "heterogeneous, disparate elements" [DEL 05, p. 507] and only preserves "that which increases the number of connections" [DEL 05, p. 508], always changing as actions are carried out and events take place. The consistency at stake in my proposal is something that holds throughout life, despite actions and events. According to these readings, changes in state seem to prevail over the entity, which is somehow buried and marginalized. For example, Deleuze and Guattari write, "Figures are considered only from the viewpoint of the *affections* that befall them" [DEL 05, p. 362]. This is what is taken up in unambiguous terms by a commentary on Deleuze's anthropology, according to which "a body is not a thing, a substance, it does not have real outlines, and it exists only in that it affects and is affected" [ZOU 94, p. 101]. Following the same logic, the entity theorized by Bruno Latour cannot be defined otherwise: through its relations, through the action with which it modifies an object or is affected by this action. It seems described, and it looks like it exists at each moment only in its unfolding in connection with other entities. As Latour writes[22], "each entity can only be defined through its relations. If the relations change, the definition follows suit"

---

21 I confess that I sometimes wonder whether fluxes or lines, those of Deleuze-Guattari or Ingold, are within a living being, outside and emanating from him, or whether they constitute the living being himself, as we can also read.

22 In other works [PIE 14a, PIE 16], I have commented in this respect on Bruno Latour's point of view.

[LAT 94]. It is as if, in this case, there were "modes of existence", in Bruno Latour's words, but without existing beings and without specific consistency. Therefore, a major risk is to "drop" the entity and regard as unsuitable and nearly repressed[23] a focus on the unity and entirety of a human volume, whose affection is only one element. Action, freedom, choice: Sartrean and existentialist works in general had a specific lexical mark. The mark of Deleuze's philosophy is not the same. It is above all flux, becoming, heterogeneity and affection that are at the center. In both configurations, relation is a central element.

3. Flux is an important topic in contemporary philosophy. Undoubtedly, Giorgio Agamben is not reluctant to conceive and even highlight individual singularities[24]. Yet, what strikes me in Agamben's proposals is their own temptation to dilute being. Thus, he writes that "being does not pre-exist the modes but constitutes itself in being modified, is nothing other than its modification" [AGA 16, p. 170], that it is "a flux" or "incessant emergence", and that singular existence is "an infinite series of modal oscillations, by means of which substance always constitutes and expresses itself" [AGA 16, pp. 172-173]. This is one of the risks involved in emphasizing modes as a "demand of being" [AGA 16, p. 170] to the extent that it may be said that "substance is its modifications" [AGA 16, p. 174]. The volume undergoes microvariations, but it cannot be forgotten that he is also a clearly constituted unity that remains always distinguishable from them when they occur and pervades them. I would like to emphasize all these terms. Agamben comments on and critiques Aristotle. On the contrary, I think that his *Metaphysics* is a good point of reference to conceive the human being as a separate volume with his consistency[25]. As Aristotle points out, "It is true that man is a principle of man at the universal level, but there is no universal man in reality. Rather it is Peleus that is the motive cause of Achilles and your father that is yours" [ARI 04, p. 306]. By this, I would like to recall that the volume is "matter" that is always already intrinsically associated with a "form", as has been pointed out – this is what constitutes the volume since he emerges as unique cell – and therefore that at each moment there is a

23 This is the word used in [DEL 80, p. 456] to refer to the situation of the so-called "ambulant sciences", which highlight flux and movement. This is no longer the case today, given that the epistemology of flux has become significantly more important. The human entity, on the contrary, is always neglected.
24 The book I refer to, *The Use of Bodies*, can attest to that [AGA 16].
25 See the references to Aristotle in *Le Volume humain* [PIE 17]. I found Pierre Aubenque's [AUB 09] reading and interpretation very useful.

continuity that manifests itself in the volume, who volumuates while also absorbing and regulating what happens, and that there is a "form" complexified by various voluments, a consistency and especially a style that provides in its own way structure and unity. The crucial degree of the force of continuity and absorption naturally differs according to the moments in life. Actions and emotions have different effects but, every time, they seem to hardly change the volume who restores his equilibrium and continues. At each moment, the consistency of the volume of being is always well acknowledged, even if it is nuanced or may be nuanced, based on volumuations of ideas, memories, gestures and know-hows. Therefore, the volume volumuates partially and also determines his modalities of change. I find it significant that Agamben notes with regret that "maneries", manners, in Medieval philosophy were traced back to the Latin verb *manere*, which means remaining, and that he prefers associating them with another verb, *manare*, which indicates a flowing and even fleeing movement [AGA 16, p. 224]. What about pervading continuity or the ceaselessly creative flux? I do not think that the human volume, with what he allows to hold back, can be compared with a "flux". An anthropologist who wishes to describe a volumuating volume may do so independently of philosophical controversies, which in this respect signpost a significant part of the history of philosophy. Therefore, he starts observing the entirety of the volume over short periods of time, and his partial variations, retrieving the traces of what happens and reversible changes, and seeing then, as has already been suggested, what remains identical and what changes temporarily or lastingly, from one situation to another, and also how what changes may be pervaded by what remains and by various pervading voluments. Indeed, there is no perfect stability or immutable identity in a volume. There are partial volumuations like molts, but there is a fully developed consistency and well-established voluments, which continue – some of which are on hold – go through the volume, and mark other voluments, including what may be experienced as ruptures or discontinuities. Therefore, I think it is important to carry out volumuographies of the same volumes at different time intervals in order to accurately measure continuity and change, beyond the feelings of continuity or the impressions of discontinuity, over periods of 10, 20 or 30 years. These points, which may seem related to old metaphysical issues, on the contrary seem to me to represent a jump forward in the empirical history of anthropology.

3.4. Intersubjectivity

1. Recent research, carried out, for example, by Joao de Pina-Cabral [PIN 17a] or Christina Toren [TOR 12], indicates an emphasis on the individual, subjectivity and even his uniqueness in anthropology. The notion of relation is also being interestingly critiqued, for example, in *World*, a recent book by Pina-Cabral [PIN 17a, p. 172 and ff]. However, this reflection hinges on intersubjectivity and therefore on the presence and importance of the others, without actually analyzing the volume as such or distancing itself from the fieldwork or classical ethnography and its expectations. My remarks are indeed reductive and do not wish in any way to diminish the intellectual force of the analyses in question, whose direction is quite a rarity in anthropology. Naturally, it is difficult to reject the idea that "involvement with other people is a necessary condition for everyone's emergence as 'self'" or that "intersubjectivity is a necessary condition for the emergence of subjectivity" [PIN 17b], in Joao de Pina-Cabral's words, and it would be a mistake to reject it. However, this idea may be nuanced. For example, I would like to draw attention to Winnicott's ideas, in particular the ability of a young child to withdraw himself and be alone, which uphold the hypothesis of a sort of "isolate, permanently non-communicating" dimension in everyone [WIN 12, p. 187]. Therefore, as I have pointed out, I think that lessereity and the minor gestures that everyone makes, which have nothing to do with the stakes of the relation in progress, are an expression of this permanent withdrawal from others and collective stakes and a necessity in the others' mode of appropriation. Additionally, the (partially) intersubjective constitution of the individual should not rule out a focus on the human volume, in particular in order to better observe and understand this constitution in its details as well as the absorbing consistency of the volume and its unitary structuration, which does not seem a "dividuality" to me. Like the "book volume", the human volume has in a certain sense his own binding and way of structuring himself. Rather, he acts as an individuality that maintains itself as such, expresses itself as such, holds itself back and restrains itself as such, with its pervading voluments and its lessereity. I have emphasized this point several times. Based on this idea of intersubjectivity or its synonyms, most anthropologists immediately focus only on intersubjectivity, situating the volume in past or present interactions, relations and connections. An emphasis on the interdependence between the volumic unity and the others, and on the outside as explanatory factor, prevails then over the observation of the entity and the way it structures itself.

2. Francisco Varela's theoretical ideas and some interpretations of his work clarify in their way the point I have just mentioned: a hesitation between a focus on unity and a focus on intersubjectivity, or more generally between the unity as it is foregrounded and the unity with the other (or the world). This point crops up in *Principles of Biological Autonomy*, on the biological scale of the book. Working with biological systems, for example, cells, and putting forward like a biologist a set of concepts – in particular the notion of autopoiesis – employed to conceive the living unity, Francisco Varela writes that "unity (the fact of being distinguishable from the environment, and hence from other unities) is the only necessary condition for existence in any given domain" [VAR 89, pp. 61–62][26]. Therefore, Varela defines autopoietic systems as follows: they "produce their identity [and] they distinguish themselves from their environment: this is why they are called autopoietic, from the Greek *autos* (self) and *poiein* (to produce)" [VAR 89, p. 45]. With the boundaries that delimit it [VAR 89, pp. 84, 86], unity is distinguishable from "its background" [VAR 89, p. 190] and remains "a unity […] independently of the changes it may undergo". Unities of this kind have an "individuality", stability, coherence and identity [VAR 89, p. 47 and p. 88], which are regarded as internal. Varela insists on this internal coherence, considering the absorption and regulation of disruptions as being in the service of the organization of the unity. This "closure" certainly does not involve shutting out the outside world [VAR 89, p. 217]. In this reading, unity is not defined by the other or by external things [VAR 89, p. 7]. This is indeed how I would conceive the observation and analysis of the human volume. Varela's target is unity, with its own organization, and the surface of coupling, as he points out, only constitutes a part of the whole [VAR 89, p. 191]. He spells it out again: "The term 'closure' refers to the fact that the result of an operation is situated within the boundaries of the system itself" [VAR 89, p. 217]. Varela sees this closed unity as "a system significantly defined from the inside" [VAR 89, p. 192] and associates it with the image of a "snake biting its own tail" [VAR 89, p. 8] or the idea of "coming full circle" [VAR 89, p. 19]. Similarly, on his scale, the volume of being makes it possible to draw attention, as has been noted, to the fact that it is within him that voluments – which have different requirements in the constitution of the empirical unity – develop, establish themselves or change, lessening and only modifying him partially from situation to situation. Considering the unity in its internal cohesion rather than based on "points of contact" between different unities [VAR 89, p. 192]

---

26 The citation pages, translated into English, are from the French edition [VAR 89].

does not imply in both cases, as Varela explains, the same "common thread" [VAR 89, p. 192] or the same "point of view" [VAR 89, p. 197]. As he points out, various types of research may be compared according to the importance they attach to the identity of a system, its interactions with what it is not and the modes of relation through which they structure these two aspects [VAR 89, p. 9]. I freely adapt this idea, noting that these three possibilities may be called on even in anthropology, but that in its history, the first is rare, since the social sciences and social anthropology focus on events or interactions instead of the human unity itself. As I have claimed, this is typically an issue addressed by existantial anthropology: following the unity beyond its events, actions and relations. Therefore, it could be heuristic to reconsider Varela's line of thinking about the living unity as separate from its environment, with its internal structuration and its possible deformations, which it self-compensates, in the face of the outer world and the others. However, I feel questioned by some points. It seems to me that Varela's theory tends to emphasize a "production" dimension of the unity, presented as an "assertion of one's own identity" [VAR 89, p. 7] or a "self-assertion" [VAR 89, p. 192]. Thus, Varela regards the unity as "a network of processes that produce components" that "regenerate ceaselessly through their transformations" [VAR 89, p. 45]. Varela seems to consider his unity in an "active role", which produces and ensures its identity and coherence. Production, regeneration, transformation: I think that these terms, which are typical of interpretations in terms of autopoiesis and can therefore adopt an "actionist" angle, are out of keeping with what a human being reveals, all the more so if in some cases they conceive this movement as creativity or emancipation. Naturally, the human volume acts, but he is always mixed with a passive component: he is inexorably associated with stylistic marks that appropriate what happens to him, but I cannot emphasize enough the lessening dimension that pervades everything originating from or happening to the volume. The theory of the volume does not separate the identity of the volume from how he retains his actions, and it emphasizes the lessening re-appropriation not only of what occurs externally but also of his internal volumuations. There is another pitfall that the theory of the volume tries to avoid: always being at the borderline of the focus on the entity, following a thread that leads to another point of view. Just as they spell out this assertion of identity, Varela's remarks concern unities that are always open and also presented in connection with environments, "relatively independently" of what surrounds them [VAR 89, p. 190]. There is indeed a distinct unity, but there is also "the necessity of the number two" [VAR 89, p. 190]. This creates, or in any case opens up, the possibility of conceiving less the unity itself than the "coupling" between the unity and its environment or the "interlinked history of their structural transformations, where each chooses the other's trajectories" [VAR 89, p. 64]. Depending on the circumstances, Varela notices then that "the behavior of a unity is a function of the behavior of other unities" [VAR 89, p. 81] and observes some "reciprocal changes undergone by the unities during their interactions" [VAR 89, p. 81] or the organization of a unity seen as subordinate to its environment and other unities [VAR 89, p. 82]. Therefore, at the end of *Principles of Biological Autonomy*, Varela establishes that "our world and our actions are inseparable" and claims to look for a middle path, the point where "the co-emergence of unities and their worlds take shape" [VAR 89, p. 224]. The importance attached to the initial unity seems indeed to be nuanced by the status left to the others and the environment. A double separate focus or multiple separate focuses would undoubtedly be methodologically ideal in anthropology: observing all humans but separately, each in his separate continuity. However, according to the consistency of the volume at each moment, I would not regard his relations or attempted relations as "structural transformations". There are only volumuations in a consistency that appropriates and lessens. Too much production and too much interdependence: the "autopoietic" reading faces some limitations in order to observe the human volume. Therefore, in *Principles of Biological Autonomy*, different alternatives of focus can be found again. First, there is a focus on the unity, the human volume, regardless of what he does or does not do, targeted in his stability and coherence, as the rest is relegated to the background: this is what I wish to prioritize. Second, the focus on the human unity can immediately be limited to moments and places of "coupling" and connections with the world or the others: in this case, the goal can be to understand a volume who, however, is fragmented, as Varela will by targeting the cognition embodied in sensorimotor structures according to situations and thinking that "what counts as pertinent world cannot be separated from what forms the structure of the perceiving subject" [VAR 04, pp. 30–31]. This nearly amounts to re-establishing the inseparability of beings and environments, while also losing the entirety of the volume. Third, the interconnection, interaction and coupling between unities may generate a superior unity [VAR 89, p. 82], which then becomes the focus instead of the basic unities, so that Varela may even think about transposing the analysis he carries out on a cellular level to the scale of different social systems [VAR 89, pp. 90–91]. Accordingly, on a methodological level, he also emphasizes the inseparability of subject and object and their interplay, where the former is in some sort coupled with the latter, and recalls then that no reality may be a "preestablished given" and that "our interpretations derive from our common history as living beings and social individuals" [VAR 89, p. 31][27]. Therefore, the temptation to lose the distinct unity and foreground the background again is always present. Does Varela's line of thinking actually not emphasize this direction or in any case highlight the interdependences of unities and environments, the codetermination of the former and the latter, interconnections with increasingly vaguer boundaries, or even an absence of separation? This implies in any case some shifts in focus: on to a self-organizing system, its opening, one of its parts in relation with the world, the interdependence itself with the environment, and therefore also the non-separation between the unity chosen and what surrounds it. In the study of the human volume, anything but him, regardless of what it is, is secondary, and I would say "blurred". I think that this is more than a methodological remark, since it is the volume himself that, through his separation and because of his way of lessening the others, holding himself back, and decoupling himself, legitimates, if I may say so, the observer to focus on the volume.

2.1. Christina Toren's anthropological analyses, which refer, among others, to Varela's ideas, do not actually manage to avoid this shift away from the unity, specifically from the human unity, towards the others, by focusing on intersubjectivity. Her line of thinking seems to rely on the uniqueness of individuals, and I find this point very significant. Thus, she insists on the history of every individual: "our uniqueness [...] is given in the fact that each one of us has a personal history that makes us who we are" [TOR 12, p. 25]. I fully subscribe to these remarks:

> We are not accustomed, perhaps, to giving much thought to our bodily substance, to the actual workings of his bounded entity we call 'I'. But if you pause to think about it, you realize that what is remarkable about this bounded entity is that, like all other living things, we humans are autopoietic systems. [TOR 02, p. 115]

---

27 Between the physicochemical and the biological scale, the cellular unity scale, the cognitive scale, centered on the microprocesses of the act of perception or any other fragmentation, and the sociological scale, with its social mechanisms and collective entities, it is once again as if there were no room on an anthropological scale for human unity.

What makes me think is then the gap between these theoretical remarks, which could motivate an observation of the human being, and the ethnographic practice, for example in relation to children, in particular in rituals in Fiji. Analyzing the "transformations" of the processes involving the attribution of meaning, categories or ideas, "as historical products constituted in and through particular forms of social relations" [TOR 02, p. 122] (for example, the idea of hierarchy or God, in children of different ages, based on a participant observation and the analyses of drawings, written documents and interviews) is incontestably important. However, I think that the force of the aforementioned theoretical possibilities enables quite different modalities of observation. I would like to recall that one of the key points of the theory of the volume is exactly looking closely, on the one hand, at some voluments, thoughts, or ideas as they modify and nuance themselves (whereas other voluments and thoughts, at the same moment, are not concerned) and, on the other hand, at the presence of more stabilized voluments, like style, marking with their traits what happens in the volume. If I want to consider everyone's uniqueness seriously and understand the regulation modes of the system constituted by each human entity, and for example, some of Varela's ideas on the separate unity, it is indeed a precise observation scale, based on the anthropological volume, that we need in order to establish volumuations, continuities, the genealogy of a style and point out the modes of appropriation of the others' voluments in a volume, instant after instant and situation after situation. While it seemed so evident in the theoretical framework put forward by Christina Toren, this detailed focus on the volume himself and his ontogenesis in course seems to have been put on hold. Why? The awkwardness of looking at the human being? I think that the answer here lies also in the theoretical importance that C. Toren attaches, in this construction of the individual, to the "others", more precisely to "intersubjective relations with others" [TOR 12, p. 25] included "in a long history of social relations" [TOR 12, p. 13] – "to all those others (young and old, living and dead) whose ideas and practices are contributing to structure the conditions of his or her present" [TOR 12, p. 25]. Her key point is the following: "Human autopoiesis is grounded in sociality" [TOR 02, p. 111]. Therefore, Christina Toren expresses her point of view in the following terms:

> Our intersubjective relationship to one another is always bound to be historically prior because, whenever we encounter one another, we do so as carriers of our own, always unique, history. [...] The human being whose ideas and practices we are

trying to understand and explain is social through and through and the world of people and things that this human inhabits crucially informs his or her entire constitution. [TOR 12, p. 25]

Does such an emphasis on the interdependence of beings and the social environment constitute a favorable theoretical condition for the observation of the human being in order to understand his intravolumic structuration? The emphasis on this extended intersubjectivity tends to replace the volume in the background. This sentence is especially evocative: "moment-to-moment encounters [...] are always and inevitably mediated by relations with others" [TOR 04, p. 223]. The challenge is yet to foreground the volume and relegate the others to the background if such observations of the human entity are to be carried out. Ethnographic approaches which aim to understand "how the children make sense of the conditions in the world created for them by adults" [TOR 12, p. 32] do not really depart from this way of putting into perspective. The scale of the volume does not belong here. It is as if this collective interdependence, the part of the others, theoretically and methodologically prevailed over the human being himself. In any case, this is my interpretation, and I will repeat the theoretical points mentioned in the theory of the volume: social constitution and the part of the dimension collectively relevant to each situation do not represent the entire volume in each of his encounters with the others; but above all the appropriation of the others' voluments involves a stylistic expression and a lessening modality and, consequently, the consistency of a volume seems always already like a form of diffuse resistance to the others. I think that these alternative points are important and necessary to free and enable in anthropology the observation of separate volumes. Thus, theory and method are essential if the goal is to look at as well as keep the volume. I will revisit a specific point: continuity is indeed indissociable from a process of "transformation", but the term "transformation" is strong, probably too strong. It seems to me that Christina Toren emphasizes more this "transformational" aspect than the element of "continuity": "your continuity through time is that of a dynamically transforming system" [TOR 12, p. 26], or: "any given human is [...] the transforming product of the past he or she has lived" [TOR 12, p. 25], but also: "Throughout our lives, our active engagement in the world of people and things effects continuing differentiation of the processes through which we know what we know" [TOR 12, p. 25]. This may not be a coincidence, as it is indeed the whole "system", as I would say, that it is important to observe in a detailed manner.

A continuous and detailed observation of a volume, who appears always already separate from the others, reveals his astonishing consistency, which does not really imply over time a "differentiation" of the volume from himself. On the contrary, beyond his volumuations, it is his consistency and his pervading voluments that hold him back in his continuity as he is lessening the effect of the presence of the others and their voluments within him, integrating and thus absorbing the possible microchanges due to the others and the world. Lessening the others in the volume: this may be what anthropologists do not wish to see and what a continuous observation can reveal. I believe that describing and understanding this in detail can only become truly possible by pushing to its extreme the volumuographic observation of a human being, who is then brought out from what surrounds him, as Varela might have said at some point. As I have indicated, basic anthropologicality consists of observing as directly as possible, step by step, the volume and his slowly unfolding existence. When applied to children, the volumuographic exercise becomes even more significant. Come to think of it, how can ontogenetic analyses be carried out outside volumuographies, namely continuous films (for 3, 4, 10, 12 or more hours, at regular intervals for several years, if possible) focused on an entire volume or various separate volumes? Volumuography looks at a human being directly and straightforwardly, with his capacity to continue with variations that affect specific voluments but not others, as has been noted, at different paces, to different degrees, and with different consequences, according to the moments during childhood and the capacity to change more and then to change less in the face of those elements to which children are exposed, as C. Toren mentions. In anthropology, is a continuist method that focuses on the volume without losing him to the advantage of the "others" and the surrounding background possible? I think that this implies a shift away from the recurrence of certain schemes and analytical focuses – such as intersubjectivity, relation, difference, alterity – in keeping with the right-thinking discourses favored by universities – which can be identified in the intellectual anthropological traditions found in this book. This indeed holds true regardless of the authors I have just mentioned.

2.2. Recording the existence of a volume, with on-board cameras, various detectors, and other sensors, is less unfeasible than we think. I have no doubt that this will become gradually simpler in the coming years and decades. This is an issue, but not the only one, for the anthropology of the human beings. The digitization of existence, what everyone sees, hears, encounters and moves towards, is on the scientific horizon, and this is already possible thanks to various types of software employed for personal or professional uses. An anthropologist may then confront the "author" of these various writings or recordings with his own traces and stimulate his reflective feedback (see [CAH 10]). On a different scale, as has been said above, the traces of actions or emotions marked in a diary, for example, may be followed, and some effects may be identified long afterwards. Daily notes, for example, in a professional or personal diary, which are as direct as possible and not part of a retrospective account, represent in fact a crucial volumuographic document, provided that they are detailed and concern as many voluments as possible[28]. However, this is pertinent to my point only in relation to the idea that these materials written by a human being represent his direct trace and are pervaded by the style of this volume and his own "coherence". It is well known that it is important to follow a human being, but not because he is the trace of other things and the indication of social and psychological dimensions, actions and practices. In my approach, the idea is to keep track of some notes because they are the trace of a human being who has written them.

3.5. Perspections of the individual

1. One could still object to me that a specific individual is sometimes chosen as a direct and explicit topic to be observed and analyzed in social anthropology, and that there are some studies that present "portraits", with varying levels of details and a more or less regular focus on the volume in question. The answer is clear. A focus on the individual whose actions, relations and social situations are relegated to the background, in order to understand a human entity in itself and its own structuration, constitutes the opposite of a focus on the individual situated in a social context, where the goal is to understand actions, activities, relations and situations. This is the reversal mentioned in the introduction. Jan Patrick Heiss notes a key point [HEI 15a, pp. 241–251] – to which the reader may refer – based on Biehl's research on Catarina [BIE 05], Crapanzano's research on Tuhami [CRA 80] or Wikan's on Suriati [WIK 90]. I can see here the ways in which the human being is circumvented, his reduction to a few voluments, and his dilution,

---

28 I would like to point out my mourning diary (which I kept for nearly 5 years) and the analyses I carried out on it in two books (*Le Temps du deuil* and *Détails d'amour*). On a different level, readers may refer to an article by Nigel Rapport that analyzes a series of conversations with a single individual, the topics discussed, their developments and their interrelations [RAP 99].

just as I mentioned them in section 3.1. The objective of these studies is to work with an individual to discover how he experiences a specific situation in a given social or cultural context. In these examples – others may also be mentioned – when the individual is chosen as a topic, he is immediately situated in sociocultural contexts that constitute a piece of data that may remain secondary, as I suggest, but which are essential in the anthropological tradition itself. The goal at first is not to describe the human entity as such but, on the one hand, to understand – since this entity is a mere pretext to this end – a role or a specific experience, which may sometimes be traumatic, a social situation or a social trajectory, but also cognitive or psychological characteristics, the specificity of ordinariness and everyday life, and, on the other hand, besides all this, to shed light on the diversity of the social and cultural realities of present-day reality. This is what the word "perspection" refers to: an individual is looked through so that he is put into perspective[29]. The human being is an astonishing entity in the sciences. It is possible to work on a cell to understand a cell, or a city and an institution to understand a city or an institution. However, we look at the human being in search of other things. He is in some sort intrinsically "scalable". Regarding the human being as a volume opposes exactly this "scalability" by looking and analyzing the volumic entity. Thus, in some works carried out in social anthropology, the methodological interest assigned to an individual in particular, called by his name, does not ultimately lie in the fact that he is a human being whose singularity and volumic entirety should be grasped, but in the fact that he experiences a specific experience, carries out a specific action, experiences social conflicts and belongs to a social system or a culture, which end up as the entities to understand. Possible descriptions, which may create literarily a realistic effect, are then inserted into an account or a reconstructed "story". The limitations of perspection may be supplemented by a risk of diluting the volume himself, due to the prominence accorded by the anthropologist, even in his writings and descriptions, to his own relation to the individual in question, rather than the detailed understanding of the volume observed by the researcher. As I have pointed out above, the method that employs life stories and biographies has its own methodological specificities, which do not involve looking for the details of each moment and focusing on life as it happens. Often employed in the history of anthropology, such a method does not primarily aim to understand the human volume and his empirical entity, but specific experiences, particular modes of life or social transformations, often in

---

29 See Chapter 2 on the idea of perspective.

connection with salient facts in clearly marked cultural environments in order to make up "stories". Working with various discourses or documents could not imply other interpretations and results [HEI 15b]. It is as if, nearly automatically, an anthropologist changed scales when dealing with a human volume. Observing an individual and considering him in his activities is only a methodology employed to understand other things than the volume himself, or the background rather than the figure, as I have pointed out. Naturally, the "portrait" approach does not immediately "put together" an individual with others. The focus remains to some extent on the individual. This methodological leap of scale, aimed at understanding social situations and cultural specificities, is made possible by the principle that underlies to this day, whether implicitly or explicitly, several works in social anthropology or ethnology: the principle of homogeneity or shared identity, whereby common characteristics are shared among the members of the same social and cultural group, so that it is possible to justify an interest in the individual as the representative of a group, a social situation, or a culture[30]. As I have pointed out above, immediately defining the volume as unique because of his volumage is the opposite of such a starting point. The only possible leap of scale, claimed by existantial anthropology or the anthropology of the volume, can be made through the comparisons of separate individuals, with the aim of better understanding the human species.

2. We can see that considering the individual to be the starting point is by no means a guarantee. Naturally, thinking on the basis of individuals and establishing immediately their difference and singularity [RAP 03, RAP 15] is a significant point, but the requirement of a focus on the human volume implies not only accentuating this approach and pushing it to its extreme (or avoiding losing the volume in scale shifts) but also not going through him straight away from a philosophical, political or ideological viewpoint, which guides and filters the observation and the analysis to an excessive degree. This type of filter, regardless of the type of philosophy employed, is sometimes directly marked, as has been seen before, and perhaps too much. This is typically the case, based on references, for example, to Nietzsche or Stirner, in some works by Nigel Rapport, and undoubtedly in the way in which he sometimes presents the human being as a "center of energy" who transcends societies, according to his terminology – which, incidentally, reveals how difficult it is to conceive the human being independently of societies. It is not easy to accept a definition of this kind if the goal is indeed

---

30 For a critique of this point of view, see [PIE 96, Chapter 2] and [PIE 15].

to look at the reality of the human volume as he continues on. This is the case not only because strictly speaking there are no societies to "transcend" – empirically, there are only unique human volumes, who are indeed exposed instant after instant to what happens around them and cannot naturally be reduced to classifications, as Nigel Rapport himself would say – but also because there is always a characteristic amount of activity and passivity in the volumes' modes of presence, as has been shown, whereas Rapport especially emphasizes the element of creativity, freedom and will. In addition, everyone's volumage, as the specific compresence of voluments, contributes quite significantly to his way of existing, being active–passive and continuing. What I mean to say is that the specificity of the volumage, his style in particular – I want to emphasize this point – is key for his way of coming across and integrating what happens and also of creating or taking the initiative. Besides, as I have already mentioned, this singularity, with its details, is not irreducible to knowledge, observation and description, even if these always need to be completed. This is the direction of the anthropology of the volume. I want to truly draw attention to the risk of filtering posed by philosophical works, but especially I would like to spell out again a crucial point in the theory of the volume: regardless of the philosophical starting point admitted, observing the volume, according to the moments and the situations, encourages the anthropologist to complete, nuance, add and subtract the aspects that each philosopher has made it possible to identify. Each school of thought is often associated with a specific type of anthropology and specific ways of conceiving the individual or existence. In my opinion, philosophical approaches can be useful only as combinable tools to describe specifically the successive and even simultaneous actions and feelings of the same volume. The complexity of the density of a volume's moment of presence is at stake here. Thus, existence is the existence of a volume, with instants confirming various philosophical motifs[31]. It is indeed the mixtures in presences that make it easier to move on from a situation to another. In addition, besides the compresent voluments – feelings, actions and moods corresponding to different combined interpretations or philosophical motifs – there are always some leftovers in the volume, which somehow prevent the moment from being total and help it slide even more easily into another moment.

---

31 Undoubtedly, this is one of the reasons why Heidegger's series of existentials is important: they can all be called on to observe their empirical concretization in the succession and simultaneity of moments.

3. Employing the methodological argument, one may also tell me that social anthropologists are used to highlighting individuals. Some may claim that individuals are the methodological core of ethnography. It is from this point of view that some anthropologists sometimes observe a single person, claiming to be focusing on this scale but moving past it, as has been noted, while they try precisely to shed light on social and cultural situations based on the individual. In general terms, proximity to the individuals is established as a key point typical of ethnographic know-how [PIE 16, pp. 37–38]. The anthropologist's conversation with people, his relations with a specific person, his willingness to listen, his more or less participant presence in their life, his encounters with the others or the Other, as is sometimes said, his place in social relationships, his own emotions or affects and the ethical stakes involved have long been regarded as aspects that play a crucial role in the ethnographer's knowledge and understanding. However, once again this is knowledge and understanding of actions, situations and sociocultural phenomena. It is as if the methodological humanism of the encounter – which I deem to be highlighted too much and which, in addition, cannot found a field of study – also played a part in losing the density of human volumes to the advantage of the researchers' understanding of social relations and occasionally the researchers' story of their own experience. If ethnography is at times critiqued, it is in most cases to incorporate an even more significant relational element, the "with" people [ING 14], and thus to continue diluting the human being even more through this approach. Therefore, relationism is a constant in the history of anthropology, as Ingold would argue, through its focus on the relational dimension of actions or on the links between beings and organisms, as has been noted, through the priority given to the relational methodology used with people, and even through a way of conceiving anthropology as already associated with other fields of study. I think that the anthropological challenge, strictly speaking, is found in the opposite direction: in a focus on the beings themselves beyond their relational actions, in a methodological withdrawal and the establishment of a specific field of study. The human volume is first a reality outside the anthropologists, as has been seen. Volumography, which thus varies significantly from ethnography, focuses less on the methodological individual than on the individual as a goal. I think that in order to set detailed descriptions as the anthropologist's first requirement, a focus on a human being, be it through the naked eye or a camera, does not imply this relational play but necessitates, as soon as the anthropologist starts observing, a withdrawal and detachment force from the volume in question, who is

separate from the observer. In the same space that contains the volume observed, the microvariations that the observer may generate represent only some microvariations among others provoked by the circumstances of life and are most of the time superficial in relation to the volumic entity. This point seems important to me. Terminology and etymology reveal the necessity of observing–describing the human volume. Observing means being in keeping with what is recommended and considering attentively. The historical meanings indicate the idea of "looking attentively" and "examining carefully". This word comes from the Latin *ob-servare, servare*, which means observing, paying attention, keeping an eye on, keeping, maintaining, preserving, keeping intact and saving. The prefix *ob-* reinforces this idea, since it means "before" and implies a distance. The Latin *describere* refers to the act of copying, transcribing, delimiting and determining. The idea here is that there is something to be written and described, the human volume naturally, but also his lived experiences and feelings, as has been pointed out. The prefix *de-* indicates detachment, distance and separation, recalling the other prefix *ob-*. Observing–describing a human volume: I would like to try to suggest the word "obserscription". Thinking that the human being is a volume without the burden of the philosophical, moral or political stakes involved in other terms (such as individual, person or existence) makes it easier to create this distance and may favor a feeling of astonishment that can lead the observer to take a better look at the volume's materiality and singular unity at the same time.

3.1. If I consider the human figure and the contextual background, that is, the social situation, experience, a critical event or the environment – even if, naturally, there may be gradients in the importance attached to either – I have always the impression that the human figure becomes subordinate to the background through the perspective adopted by the anthropologist[32]. The reader understands that I cannot subscribe to this fairly widespread idea, spelled out by Marc Augé among other authors, according to which "the concrete in anthropology is the opposite of the definition of the concrete accepted by certain schools of sociological thought: something to be seen in terms of orders of magnitude from which all individual variables are eliminated" [AUG 09, p. 20]. I am aware that several anthropologists have harshly criticized what I have called cultural ethnography, much more so in

---

32 It would be important to carry out comparisons about the nuances of this interplay between the figure and the background, according to various portraits that signpost the anthropological tradition.

the United States than in France. Lila Abu-Lughod went as far as writing that the ethnography of particulars "would necessarily subvert the most problematic connotations of culture: homogeneity, coherence, and timelessness" [ABU 91, p. 154]. Naturally, but what is practiced in its stead? An interactional ethnography in most cases[33]. What can be seen? Abu-Lughod spells it out: "Individuals are confronted with choices, struggle with others, make conflicting statements, argue about points of view on the same events, undergo ups and downs in various relationships [...]" [ABU 91, p. 154]. Thus, this involves once again actions, interactions and the social life, and it does not cause anthropology to break radically with its tradition or, as Abu-Lughod herself writes, "the historically constructed divide between the West and the non-West". I believe that it would be a costly mistake for anthropology to think that its history and distinguishing features are associated with ethnography and the concrete dimension of individuals in comparison with the other social sciences, which engage in conceptual abstractions. Let us say that anthropology has an announced interest in the human being which, however, it has never truly dared concretize.

3.2. According to all these remarks, anthropological portraits are not necessarily volumic. After the aforementioned theoretical developments, one may wonder which requirements would make it possible to describe a volume at a given instant t. What does it mean to carry out a volumography – which takes on its full meaning comparatively and with volumuographic complements realized ceaselessly and at regular intervals? This is how I would formulate these requirements – and this makes it possible to summarize much of what has been said:

– Describing a volume of being implies describing a human being such as he is immediately considered to be non-interchangeable with another being. He would be interchangeable if he were described exclusively in relation to an activity, a role or a situation, which could be someone else's situation, without entailing a different goal for the author: understanding the activity or the role in question.

– Thus, it implies not describing the volume in relation to a social role, an action, an activity, an experience or a situation. It also implies not reducing him to cognitive or emotional mechanisms, logics of action (of interaction,

---

33 I have suggested a critical comparison between cultural ethnography and interactional ethnography in relation to the loss of details and ultimately the human being in [PIE 96, PIE 15].

reflection and assessment, for example). It means attempting to express an entirety seized in its details by trying to find a balance between this entirety and its details.

– It implies describing as accurately as possible a style at a given instant t and, in his way of continuing and with his own details, a volume who acts, speaks and feels but is simultaneously worrying, laughing, thinking about different things, and making some gestures.

– It does not imply telling a delimited story in an account, with a beginning and an end, that is centered on an event, an ordeal, a crisis or an activity, as is often the case for ethnographic descriptions. On the contrary, it means presenting moments in a succession of other moments, as time goes by, that everyone experiences and leaves behind continuing without stopping and truly finishing.

– It implies assigning a place to the context and the background but without allowing them to monopolize the description. As I have repeatedly pointed out, the volume loses himself and is lost when he is absorbed by the context (for example, the social context), which brings about precisely a change in scale. This is the typical activity carried out in the social sciences. In a volumographic exercise, the human volume is considered in himself rather than as the indication or example of a situation, event or social class.

– Describing a volume implies describing him as if he were a human being rather than a rational, interpreting, cognitive, social or political being, as if he played a specific role; carried out a specific action; were a member of a specific class, group and community; or as if he constituted a point of view on things – as each of these dimensions corresponds only to certain voluments. This implies thinking that the volume constitutes all these aspects simultaneously, sometimes one aspect more than another, but that he is never only this or that aspect or this and that aspect. One sense in which the notion of volume is pertinent is its way of encouraging observers to look directly at the human being who is there.

– Describing as if dealing with a human being: but this is a human being. What is at stake is not a fiction, an "as if", even a methodological one. When a description regards a human being as rational, as a member of a specific community and as playing a certain role, living a specific experience or adopting a certain point of view, we more or less know that this being is not only rational, not only a member of this community, not only playing this role or living this experience and not only adopting this point of view. It is as if this characteristic constituted the entire human being. In fact, it is only a part of him and it is generally not pushed to its extreme. A being is more than rational and more than the role he plays or the activity he carries out, the experience he lives, or the point of view he adopts. He is also not totally rational or the role he plays, not totally the activity he carries out, the experience he lives and the point of view he adopts. This is what describing volumes attempts to express, and fragmenting into cognition, action or intersubjectivity prevents. This methodological fiction makes everything less exact, while describing the volumes of being increases the level of accuracy.

– Describing a volume implies looking at him according to what I think are his "basic characteristics". Thus, what characterizes a human volume is being separate from all other beings and objects, constituting an indivisible unity, being singular and not interchangeable with others, and equipped with a certain awareness and perception of his singularity, continuing while also remaining the same, and knowing that he is therefore continuing in time and penetrated by details that indicate somehow an incomplete action. Therefore, describing a human being means attempting to seize him in the succession of moments and situations. When looking at such a succession, it is impossible not to be struck by a certain facility in continuity, a somewhat detached way of being and precisely a way of not truly bringing the present situation to completion and moving on to the following. And it would be even more astonishing if this did not happen in these terms. It is necessary to focus on the continuity of moments and situations in order to observe accurately this manner of being a human being, which is specific to everyone. Indeed, when this does not occur, it is the sign of a difficulty and of a psychological or social ordeal. Even during this ordeal, there is always this human way of continuing. This feature often remains unthought in descriptions. If a description aims to be precise, it cannot neglect this aspect, which is, however, quickly lost in research, hardly seen and noticed, since it is so trivialized, and meaningless, since the social sciences are used to focus on other things. Describing a human necessarily involves reintroducing these details and seizing continuity instant after instant.

Further Development: Structural Existantism

4.1. Lévi-Strauss and the difficult ambition of anthropology

1. The social sciences are sciences of the collective. They can hardly be expected to be otherwise. They are what they are, whether they adopt Durkheim's stance (focusing on shared behaviors considered collectively outside the individuals, as Durkheim repeats), concentrate on mutual actions among individuals, their communications, their points of view on the situation, or relate to these aspects subjectivities with and intersubjectivities. "Sameness", "inter-ness", "as-ness" and "with-ness" accumulate so that the human entity itself is put into brackets. Faced with this entity, this book bets precisely that anthropology can exist without being social or cultural, relying on a different expertise from that of psychology or biology. Based on the findings of Chapter 3 and the theoretical discussions that come before it, it seems to me that, in order to be seized, the human being must be removed from some perspectives: the social and ecological contexts, intersubjectivity and the relations among organisms, and the "others" in any form, but not only. Lines, flux, wrenching away, being ahead, going beyond: I have the impression that I can find what philosophers say about the human being in the way he is anthropologically circumvented. Thus, regarding the human being as a volume and looking at him in his entirety is an approach met by various strong forms of resistance, whether theoretical, historical, institutional or ideological. Now, I would like to consider something that may seem unexpected, that is, Lévi-Strauss' ideas. Why can this analysis of the volume turn to Lévi-Strauss? There are two reasons: the anthropological goal that Lévi-Strauss ceaselessly asserted and the

suggestion of a structural method that aims to delimit an "object". For this second point, I find the structural method that I freely employ useful for keeping the volume as the central figure and deciphering his density made of voluments, in the face of some philosophical influences based on phenomenology, existentialism and their fragmentary and diluting effect. It is indeed to indicate this distance from the existentialist influence that I associate existantial anthropology with a form of structural existantism. The two points will help me continue to shed light on my topic, and I will remain critical of both. Calling on Lévi-Strauss for the description of the human being is in any case a paradoxical challenge, when it is known to which extent he thought that anthropology, in order to become a science, had to involve putting humans, individuals and subjectivities into brackets. I will go on a rather long journey through Lévi-Strauss' work, as it gives a strong and radical expression to anthropology, perhaps the strongest and most radical ever since its birth. However, it simultaneously embodies the history of anthropology, the one that preceded it and the one that followed it, with its stubbornness and limitations, in particular in relation to this focus on the human being. I see Lévi-Strauss' line of thinking as simultaneously close to and far from what may constitute the anthropology of the human beings. It is in a sort of attraction–repulsion regarding this goal. This digression on Lévi-Strauss allows me nearly to follow anthropology as it moves towards and against the human being. It will also allow me to clarify again the reversal constituted by a direct focus on the human being – this reversal is also in relation to Lévi-Strauss himself.

2. Who is then this human in the face of cultural diversity? This is a question that Lévi-Strauss asked, thereby assigning a clear objective to anthropology. His answer is not centered on the observation of the human being himself, but on his productions, specifically kinship systems, myths and totems. As it is well known, he discovered the constant of the structural unconscious, an intra-human layer able to organize social and cultural life. This involves an unconscious activity of the mind, which imposes logical forms to a content. And "these forms are fundamentally the same for all minds – ancient and modern, primitive and civilized" [LEV 63, p. 21]. It is indeed a volument of the human being that Lévi-Strauss discovers: a human, reintegrated into nature and almost into cerebral biology, in any case conceived according to cognitive capacities and the mind's structuring principles. In fact, while only a small part of the volume, this is an ideal goal and an extraordinary objective for anthropology. Besides this result, let us follow Lévi-Strauss and dissect his anthropological way of thinking.

Lévi-Strauss achieves his goal of an archaeology of the human being through his desire to discover "other" societies, lamenting the fact that he did not live "in the age of *real* travel, when the spectacle on offer had not yet been blemished" [LEV 61, p. 44]. These are his words:

> The Nambikwara social structure is essentially fluid. Bands are constantly forming and being dissolved, doubling their numbers or disappearing altogether. A few months may suffice for their composition, numbers, and general character to change beyond recognition. Domestic political intrigues and conflicts between neighbour bands impose their separate rhythms upon these variations, and both individuals and groups pass from zenith to nadir, and vice versa, in a way that is often disconcerting. [LEV 61, pp. 300–301]

Lévi-Strauss thinks that the Nambikwara live under "one of the most indigent of all conceivable forms of social and political organization" [LEV 61, p. 310]. He also adds: "I had been looking for a society reduced to its simplest expression. The society of the Nambikwara had been reduced to the point at which I found nothing but human beings" [LEV 61, p. 310]. These remarks seem very significant to me. They make me wonder whether it is truly other societies that Lévi-Strauss is looking for. He points out: "The ethnographer [...] strives to know and estimate his fellow-men from a lofty and distant point of vantage: only thus can he abstract them from the contingencies particular to this or that civilization" [LEV 61, p. 58]. The goal of anthropology is here clearly defined.

2.1. Therefore, Lévi-Strauss' proposal includes everything that does not concern ethnography, which tries precisely to understand and observe contexts and societies and is consequently in contrast with a possible and radical goal of anthropology and Lévi-Strauss' aforementioned remarks. Yet, Lévi-Strauss also describes societies and contexts. In fact, despite the author's reservations about exotic adventures, *Tristes Tropiques* fashions ethnographic descriptions of societies, power relationships, social relationships and the role of deaths, rituals, environments and body painting. The book includes nearly all the research topics that are still commonly studied today by ethnographers, most of whom remain focused on the difference between "them" and "us". Lévi-Strauss does not avoid this difference but, on the contrary, he immerses himself in it, faced with "others", whom he constantly considers, relativizes, judges and does not judge.

2.2. We thus run the risk of forgetting this human archaeology, which is so central, according to Lévi-Strauss himself, for anthropology. In losing this objective, which it can only keep explicitly and overtly, anthropology loses its distinguishing feature. This, in any case, is my opinion. Here is what Dan Sperber, a recipient of the Claude Lévi-Strauss prize, said in this respect in the speech he gave on June 29, 2009 at the Académie des Sciences Morales et Politiques:

> Claude Lévi-Strauss has made anthropology appealing for several generations of brilliant students who without him would have walked down the path of philosophy, history, or sociology. Most of them have become remarkable field researchers. Thanks to them, French anthropology is today in a leading position on a global level. Few of them, for example Maurice Godelier, Françoise Héritier, or Philippe Descola, have dedicated a significant part of their work to anthropological theory. It is true that Lévi-Strauss' theoretical corpus was somewhat intimidating. Personally, perhaps due to rashness or presumption, I wanted to emulate Lévi-Strauss the theoretician.

What Sperber says about French anthropology can be generalized to the traditions of other countries, including England and the United States. It is naturally possible to say that such theoretical works include a form of anthropologicality, but a general anthropologicality rather than the basic anthropologicality to which I refer. This anthropologicality takes shape in various ways. It may occur in a comparative approach based on empirical types of research, which focus on a particular dimension and a specific volument of the human being – this is the case for the works mentioned by Sperber. It may also involve the comparison of different forms of human and non-human life, the proposition of hominization scenarios and the elaboration of narratives of origin. It may also be a sort of generalization consisting of an explicit discourse[1] on the human condition, combined with empirical data. It is then necessary to recall the stages of the anthropological construction established by Lévi-Strauss: ethnography, ethnology as the synthesis of ethnographic data and anthropology as the synthesis of different forms of ethnology, including the search for constants. The problem is the gap between the first two and the third, which is very rare, as if the research

---

1 I think it is important for this reflection on the human being to be really explicit. It is in most cases absent in social and cultural anthropology works.

on social life carried out by ethnographers and ethnologists could not lead to a reflection on the human being, or as if there were an unbridgeable gap between the first two steps, focused on collective facts or social situations, and the third one as a discourse on the human being. In reality, ethnography and ethnology are not at first anthropologies. Indeed, for the anthropologists mentioned by Sperber, other anthropologists who have attempted to climb these three steps to anthropologicality, and also Lévi-Strauss, the theoretical issue remains often sociological in the broad sense of the term, as universal voluments are sought according to social activities or various relations. For Sperber, the theoretical issue is mainly associated with cognitive psychology and linguistics. Thus, there is not really a direct reflection about and based on the human being. In this case, the challenge would be then to find some universals that concern his own volumic entity. Could anthropologies constituted by ethnographic approaches only theorize a sociocultural and cognitive-linguistic human?

2.3. What should be done? I suggest that the theoretical goal of anthropology should be associated with an empirical observation of human beings, and that Lévi-Strauss' remarks about the aim of ethnography as the extraction of the human being from contextual contingencies should be reconsidered. As it has become the exact opposite, ethnography should indeed make a reversal by focusing radically on human beings instead of their social life. Ethnography would no longer be such – this term would no longer be relevant in this framework – but a volumography or a phenomenography, as I have suggested a while ago. Humans can be found everywhere at any time, and not only among the Nambikwara. As geology reminded Lévi-Strauss, "the most august of investigations is surely that which reveals what came before, dictates, and in large measure explains all the others" [LEV 61, p. 60]. Let us say that each human being is a Nambikwara, all the more so as "for thousands of years past mankind has done nothing but repeat itself" [LEV 61, p. 392]. Thus, anthropology would find its object in the human being in the strict sense of the term, since it cannot be the sociological diversity of cultures and social relations, all the more so as "primitive societies" have been lost. Anthropology can also revisit its archaeological argument in an explicit quest for primary "primitive modes" of acting and being that each human being expresses in some way [TES 86]. It is in this vein that anthropology must then find methodological alternatives, knowing that a method does not constitute a field of study, as is sometimes thought about ethnography practiced in various disciplines.

2.3.1. Due to a number of reasons that signpost the anthropological tradition, Lévi-Strauss could not truly give concrete shape to this observation of human beings, one at a time, separate from their contexts. First, there are the difficulties inherent in the humanities and the social sciences, as well as the relation they imply between the observer and those observed. Lévi-Strauss mentions this several times [LEV 96, p. 339 and ff.]. He even goes as far as writing that consciousness is "the secret enemy of the human sciences" [LEV 96, p. 344]. These difficulties could only increase and become thornier should we observe a single person and confront a single human being, who is aware of being observed, in comparison with individuals who are diluted in their activities. However, perhaps this is not the most important point. Thus, a human volume contains what Lévi-Strauss rejects in his conviction that science and its aim to be objective must go beyond the subjective and experience, which are always missed. Lévi-Strauss does not stop repeating that the ego, just like personal experience, is detestable and that true reality lies elsewhere. He writes that "to reach reality we must first repudiate experience" [LEV 61, p. 62]. He thus refers to phenomenology, rejects any analysis on the subject, whom he regards as an "unbearably spoilt child" [LEV 90, p. 687], refuses to associate the meaning of an action with the individual's awareness of it, and reproaches Sartre for starting from a naïve type of cogito, aligning consciousness with the meaning it creates, "steeping himself in the allegedly self-evident truths of introspection" [LEV 62, p. 249], and getting "lost in the blind alleys of social psychology" [LEV 62, p. 250]. Immediately after this, Lévi-Strauss reproaches Bergsonism for reducing "people and things to pap-form" [LEV 61, p. 59] and Gurvitch for his "high regard for the concrete (involving praise of its richness, complexity, fluidity, inexpressible character, and creative spontaneity)" [LEV 63, p. 326]. All this is quite well known. Of course, according to the anthropology of volumes the only form of reality is constituted by the human volume and his voluments, which an observer can observe or in any case learn to discover. However, this type of anthropology can also reassure Lévi-Strauss in some respects. As has been seen, there is no ego in a volume, but only compresences of voluments. Subjectivity as a feeling is only a volument among other voluments, which can be accessed methodologically, and the volume is far from being a flux. On the contrary, the volume is an intradetermined entity, a consistency and a density that moves fairly slowly.

2.3.2. Lévi-Strauss develops his ideas about the human being by writing that he is only "this supposed totalizing continuity of the self" and "an illusion sustained by the demands of social life" [LEV 62, p. 256], as the instants and situations that follow one another include only "cerebral, hormonal or nervous phenomena, which themselves have reference to the physical or chemical order" [LEV 62, p. 257]. He pushes his materialism to an extreme degree, indicating that he has spent his life studying "institutions, manners, and customs" [LEV 61, p. 397] whose only meaning, as he admits, lies in allowing humankind to live. These "creations", which become meaningful only in relation to "the human mind", will vanish in chaos "as soon as it ceases to exist". That is right! Lévi-Strauss continues along these lines at the end of *Tristes Tropiques*, refusing to claim that he himself exists. As an individual, he is "a constantly renewed stake in the struggle between the society, formed by the several million nerve-cells" [LEV 61, p. 397]. I am willing to acknowledge this. However, something seems strange to me. In fact, it is surprising that, confronted with the choice between human nothingness, made of cells, and the "we" that becomes meaningful only in relation to the human mind, according to his own words, Lévi-Strauss finds it obvious to study the "we" (institutions, customs), as if it had immediately more unity and consistency than the human being. Some may discuss whether it is the individual or collective systems that are ontologically prioritized. However, it is hard to remove the human individual *and* keep the two other elements, that is, cells and societies, since the latter are only a cluster of individuals who are a cluster of cells. In so doing, anthropology loses the human being, that is, this volume who is not less real than institutions. Lévi-Strauss is also indeed a sociologist, as has been seen. This is the prevailing aspect, which Lévi-Strauss cannot truly dismiss: "To be a man means for each of us membership of a class, a society, a country, a continent and a civilization" [LEV 61, p. 392]. He also very explicitly states, "Each man feels as a function of the ways in which he is permitted or obliged to act" [LEV 91, p. 70]. Besides, he assigns to institutions and collective systems an autonomy that is well established in the sociological tradition:

> If institutions and customs drew their vitality from being continually refreshed and invigorated by individual sentiments, like those in which they originated, they ought to conceal an affective richness, continually replenished, which would be their positive context. We know that this is not the case. [LEV 91, p. 70]

In addition, penetrated by the reality of the structures established by the human intellect, these institutions end up becoming more real than the human beings themselves. Nothingness and entropy are a reality, but this does not justify the fact that there are experts in cells and the collective systems invented by men but no experts in human entities. In fact, there is unity in the volume too, like in minerals, plants or insects. Either there are merely biologists and physicists or there are experts in cells and atoms, and experts in human institutions, and in this case experts in human volumes with their voluments are also required.

2.4. Following Lévi-Strauss, there are then two ways of being an anthropologist. Anthropologists may continue to explore cultural varieties and social relations according to a more or less detailed type of ethnography, which may or may not include an explicit theoretical claim. This implies, whether we like it or not, fitting in line with the sociological approach, and this is usually the case, with highly variable connections and modalities. Otherwise, anthropologists may explore the human intellect moving in the direction of a cognitive type of psychology, anchored in ethnographic research in different ways, or towards a broader type of psychology than that of the cognitive sciences, which is still, however, motivated and framed by the issue of social and cultural varieties. Thus, I return with firmer conviction to what seems to me to be the foundation of the anthropological goal: describing and comparing human beings as extracted from their contexts, societies and civilizations. This is what may be called "existantism". In order to find human beings, what could be better than looking at them without diluting them? Lévi-Strauss' work does not include this possibility, as has been seen, even if it briefly discusses [LEV 96, p. 44] the idea of the entire human, with "physical, physiological, psychical, and sociological" aspects [LEV 87, p. 26]. Unsurprisingly, Lévi-Strauss focused on the ways of classifying individuals and the divisions operated by names, and not on the volumes themselves[2]. Although Mauss – as has been seen before – immediately placed this total human in groups and related him to his activities, his social life and social systems, Lévi-Strauss refused the risks involved in subjectivity, or what he regarded as such, and preferred assigning to anthropology, based on a study of human productions and the hypothesis of the universal structural unconscious, the goal of a natural science [LEV 96, p. 29]. I think that this absence deserved the analysis I have just carried out, especially when we remember that Lévi-Strauss seemed to be glad to discover the human among the Nambikwara all the

---

2 See the chapter "The individual as a species" in *The Savage Mind* [LEV 62].

more easily as they had their strong individual differences, without a solid social organization.

4.2. A structural approach and the human volume

1. In any case, it is important to keep referring to the ideal goal of anthropology. This goal is indissociable from it, and it must be so. As has been shown above, Lévi-Strauss greatly recalls this goal, but in the end he circumvents and even refuses the human being. There is another point, just as important, in Lévi-Strauss' work, a method, a desire to systematize, formalize and seize one's object. When dealing with the human volume, the structural method may be valuable, and finding it among the ideas of anthropology is a positive thing. Thus, it is possible to keep conversing with Lévi-Strauss.

1.1. When re-reading the history of anthropology, it appears that the idea of "structure", according to different meanings, is often at the center of theories. However, the goal is not the structure of the human being, as if it were evident that it is so. Thus, this is what Ruth Benedict writes in *Patterns of Culture* before mentioning a few pages later the "Gestalt psychology":

> Cultures, likewise, are more than the sum of their traits. We may know all about the distribution of a tribe's form of marriage, ritual dances, and puberty initiations, and yet understand nothing of the culture as a whole which has used these elements to its own purpose. [BEN 60, p. 53]

Most importantly, as if it were well established that anthropology circumvents the human being, the anthropologist ends up comparing a civilization with an individual in order to understand the former: "A culture, like an individual, is a more or less consistent pattern of thought and action. Within each culture there come into being characteristic purposes not necessarily shared by other types of society" [BEN 60, p. 53]. Thus, the object of anthropology is a civilization but not the individual! In the same vein, Radcliffe-Brown puts forward the notion of "structural form" as "the continuity of social structure through time" [RAD 52, p. 192], beyond the dynamic of concrete reality and social relations. He also comparatively hints at the individual organism that is permanent and mobile throughout its life. He is interested in seizing the structure of societies, and if the individual may become relevant for a social anthropologist it is only "through the social structure", as a "position in the social structure" and a "complex of social relationships" [RAD 52, p. 194]. In the history of anthropology, a holistic view – classic and heuristic, with other objects – does not seem relevant to bring out the human figure. On the contrary, the human figure is somehow relegated to the background. It is this way due to the history of anthropology and its institutions.

1.2. To shed light on the human volume, I will not employ a specifically Lévi-Straussean type of structuralism, but levers to establish a modality for analysis and to clarify structural existantism. The structural method should be regarded as a guide that can define the human being as a research topic and source of inspiration, rather than as a form of adherence to Lévi-Strauss' theoretical frame. I insist on the idea of methodological guidance, as if the analysis of the volume and his details looked for some support that the phenomenological or existential tradition does not necessarily provide. A methodological inspiration means a reference to some general principles and not an application of the complexity of analyses of myths or kinship systems – nothing more than that, but still with necessary adjustments to Lévi-Strauss' discourse – and it also means an occasion to clarify my topic once again. I do this while keeping my aim, that is, describing the volume in detail and continuously. I will elaborate on three points in Lévi-Strauss' reflection and link them to my own line of thinking: details, the unity of the system and voluments with the issue of lived experiences, and then transformations or volumuations.

1.2.1. The first point concerns details or "leftovers". What can we read in Lévi-Strauss' works? He tells us that "All the facts should be carefully observed and described, without allowing any theoretical preconception to decide whether some are more important than others" [LEV 63, p. 280], or that he is looking for a method that can seize the "entirety of the facts observed" and that is "exhaustive", with an analysis that makes it possible to "exhaust all the concrete modalities of one's object" [LEV 64, p. 155]. Lévi-Strauss also explains that when he carries out research, he does not know beforehand the elements to which the "structural analysis can be applied" [LEV 63, p. 327], that in order to find out it is necessary to pay close attention to "details" and "the small facts", including those that at first seem "astructural" [LEV 63, p. 327], and that what is not immediately intelligible may be put aside and explained later, in reference to other pieces of information or comparisons. Yet, I should be cautious. In fact, despite what has been just noted, the empirical diversity that Lévi-Strauss refers to is undoubtedly supplanted more rapidly than he lets on, and the leftovers acknowledged once and for all as astructural are discarded. His own descriptions do not reveal a specific focus on details. Lévi-Strauss does not hide his reservations on "day-to-day observation" [LEV 61, p. 50]. It is well known that in terms of writing, any type of ethnography is a cumulative process of data loss. The structural method is not immune to it, and sometimes it can radically illustrate this. In fact, Lévi-Strauss does not really wish to favor the "leftovers" of his analyses. Indeed, he aims to extract "constants" [LEV 63, p. 82] from the complexity and diversity of empirical data through a "reduction" operation and the search for differences and relevant contrasts. Lévi-Strauss' approach, in which "the existence of differentiating features is of much greater importance than their content" [LEV 62, p. 75], retains a small number of elements in order to show contrasts and form pairs of oppositions. This type of remark can often be found in Lévi-Strauss' work, even if he occasionally claims again that "the phenomena subjected to reduction must not be impoverished; one must be certain that everything contributing to their distinctive richness and originality has been collected around them" [LEV 62, p. 247]. In any case, it seems difficult to avoid the "reduction". There is also another famous formulation by Lévi-Strauss, which is relevant to my topic: "I believe the ultimate goal of the human sciences to be not to constitute, but to dissolve man" [LEV 62, p. 247]. What does Lévi-Strauss mean by this verb, "to dissolve"? He does not mean "the destruction of the parts", as he points out: "The solution of a solid into a liquid alters the disposition of its molecules. It also often provides an efficacious method of putting them by so that they can be recovered in case of need and their properties be better studied" [LEV 62, p. 247]. As it appears, such a "solution" of a volume involves the risk of dissolving him, in particular into his "physico-chemical conditions", in Lévi-Strauss' words. On the anthropological scale on which I insist, I suggest more an extraction of the volume, so that it is possible to look at *him* and in detail. The eliminated leftovers are key for the observer of volumes, who employs it with the aim of nuancing the types of logic discovered and indicating then that the human volume is not only a structuring logic that involves classifying and shaping what surrounds him. The understanding of the volume as an entire unity and of the way in which he is structured cannot only be associated with the structural unconscious and a single capacity, in this case a cognitive one. This cognitive capacity can shed light on the logic of cultural productions but not on that of the human volume himself.

Focusing on this entire volume – an operation which keeps track of leftovers – involves observing the largest number of voluments possible, identifying different compresence dynamics among them, and adding nuancing leftovers to them. Taking into consideration the risk of loss, it is important to remember the idea of "system" as an entirety to cover. This idea encourages such an empirical requirement, which involves a search, indeed infinite but still carried out on the surface of and within the volume, for these directly retrievable leftovers and other less visible ones. It is in this vein that an anthropologist looks at a human being and will look for contact and interference modalities among the voluments mentioned above. To this end, as he is aware, he cannot forget lessereity and the details concerning the modes of presence.

1.2.2. The second point, which is significant for the anthropology of the volume, has to do with Lévi-Strauss' emphasis on the "sharpness of outline" [LEV 61, p. 59], which should not be lost and delimits beings and things. From this perspective, what interests me is the objective of considering myths or any other object as a "closed system" with its own intelligibility, besides historical or geographic explanations and the contextual ethnographic information, which are merely preliminary [LEV 96, p. 353][3]. I see in this idea of "closed system" an invitation to conceive the human being indeed not as closed but in himself and as containing his own intelligibility, which anthropology should detect, unlike various kinds of sociology, ethnology or psychology, which look for intelligibilities outside the volume or in his fragmented parts. Naturally, not resorting to ethnological or sociological explanations does not mean that there are no external elements that reach the human volume and especially that these elements do not have a certain meaning before their emergence and their entry-reception into the volume. However, in any case the anthropological focus would remain firmly on the volume and on how he handles, integrates or does not integrate these elements. All this is in a sense similar to the opposition that Saussure, at the beginning of his *Course in General Linguistics*, saw between external linguistics, which studies what lies outside language (its history, culture and institutions), and internal linguistics, which regards language as a system with its own order [SAU 98]. Yet, I think that in relation to social and cultural types of anthropology, unlike external linguistics, the various expressions of society and culture are

---

3 Just as it can shed light on mythologies, contextual data can also help us understand the volume and his voluments.

directly established as research topics rather than as explanations of the human being.

1.2.2.1. In this vein, Lévi-Strauss puts the accent once again on the importance of "the whole" or "totality" – I prefer "entirety" – of any research topic which, as he writes, is "arbitrary when only its individual terms are considered" [LEV 62, p. 54]. This is well known. I will insist on a few points. Some mythemes take on their meaning only as part of an entire myth, in their syntagmatic connections and their paradigmatic associations (by contrasting them when they emerge in successive syntagmata). Of course, some comparisons can also be drawn between several myths. It is also in an entirety and necessarily in this entirety, the human volume, that the observer identifies and decodes voluments which are real, whether they are visible or not. Sometimes they can be delimited or in any case associated with specific traits, but they cannot be separated from the volume in whom they take shape and take on their own meaning. This implies a meticulous division between the voluments of a volume. Undoubtedly, an anthropologist can adapt this division according to his data, aiming to bring together and contrast voluments that derive from a syntagmatic and horizontal line with other voluments deriving from paradigmatic and vertical lines [LEV 63, p. 210 and ff.]. However, Lévi-Strauss does not deny that terms outside their system or mythemes outside their myths have value or a meaning [LEV 63, p. 91 and ff.]. As I have just mentioned, the voluments of a volume, which of course cannot exist outside him, may still have some meaning through some of their characteristics, which can be found in different volumes and not only in their mutual effects or relations within a specific volume. For example, an emotion, gesture, facial expression and cultural trait have a general range of possible meanings or echoes. But, in a specific volume, these meanings may be refined by other particular meanings or interpretations, in connection with his other voluments. Similarly, some of these voluments, for example gestures or gestural movements, which do not seem to have at a given time t specific functions or connotations, may be compared with similar movements of the same volume at other times and explained through stylistic resemblances. In fact, it is very important to bring these voluments together in order to identify recurring dimensions in the continuity of the volume. Even though it is possible to focus closely on each volument, at a specific time, according to the anthropologist's objective, a structural approach based on the volumic unity aims especially to understand the combination of voluments and their effects, moment after moment. In a human volume, it is often some compresences of specific voluments, rather than other compresences, which are interesting to describe presences (but, as is well known, the leftovers should always be reincorporated into the description). These compresences may involve the causation, permeation, concretization, simultaneity, direction, as has been mentioned in Chapter 1. Thus, for example, when comparing a particular volume between a specific situation (which may then correspond to a syntagmatic line) and, as I have just noted, similar situations (which correspond to other syntagmatic lines), I identify favored interdependencies between voluments, recurrent combinations of specific voluments, a specific word, gesture and stylistic trait, or a specific social or cultural mark. Therefore, a specific volument of a volume, that is, a gesture or posture, can be observed in similar situations, pervaded by another volument, which is every time the same. I find it very important then to compare the syntagmatic and paradigmatic lines of the same voluments, in order to identify these interdependencies between voluments, and the modalities of these interdependences. This is what Lévi-Strauss writes about music scores:

> But after trying, without success, to decipher staffs one after the other, from the upper down to the lower, they would probably notice that the same patterns of notes recurred at intervals, either in full or in part, or that some patterns were strongly reminiscent of earlier ones. Hence the hypothesis: What if patterns showing affinity, instead of being considered in succession, were to be treated as one complex pattern and read as a whole? By getting at what we call harmony. [LEV 63, p. 212]

Is this not what I mean in this book by continuity and in particular by stylistic expressions? These repetitions of specific compresences, even more than those of isolated voluments, indicate individual tones and specific modalities of continuity for the volume in question. In a different direction, the repeated compresences of two specific voluments, in comparison with other compresences of one of these two voluments with a third, may reveal the microvariation effects of one on the other: for example, the difference of a specific gesture when a specific emotion is or is not involved, or the difference of a specific stylistic trait when this or that specific gesture is made. It is not always the same emotion, value or thought that is compresent with the same action or gesture, in the volume who is thus characterized by the mobility of the voluments. However, this does not mean that these differences do not remain pervaded by elements of the style of the volume.

These various comparisons can be identified by drawing parallels between the successive moments of the same volume but also by contrasting different volumes. I have the impression that a large empirical field is opening up about specific volumes and with the aim of making general comparisons, allowed by a structural reading, with more or less flexible applications. I should also note that in a volume, a change in one volument does not necessarily entail changes in the others, let alone in all the other voluments, in contrast with the classic definition of systems [LEV 63, pp. 279–280]. In this respect, I have significantly emphasized the continuity of the volume and of the voluments beyond their variations. In any case – I find this point particularly important, and I think that the ideas of entirety and system may help me formulate it – habits, know-hows, memories, thoughts and so on have always already their place in a volume and not elsewhere, accompanied by volumuating expressions at different paces. Similarly, when ideas or moods fluctuate, they do so only through and within the volumic unity. No volument has absolute priority. Sometimes one, sometimes the other prevails in a given moment of presence, as has been shown. It is the volume who radically comes first. Without him, there would be no voluments and several voluments do not seem necessary for him and, in any case, are only a small part of an entirety, which continues beyond the variations.

1.2.2.2. What I have just pointed out entails another consequence. As is well known, Lévi-Strauss vigorously refuses to incorporate feeling, consciousness, thoughts and emotions into his analyses. However, the notion of volume and what it implies may in a certain way relativize their place in the volume and the methodological difficulty involved in seizing them. In fact, it is the volume who contains the various voluments that we know, including his lived experiences, his feelings, his emotions and thoughts of any kind. Some interpretations may block the methodological grip of what is contained in a volume and belongs to him only. An act of consciousness is only a volument or a compresence of some voluments in the volume and, in his composition, consciousness could not be conceived, in Husserl's words, as "the only individuality", the only origin of individuality [HUS 80, p. 315]. Observing a volume, I can only see voluments among other voluments, a perception, a possible feeling or a mode of consciousness, which is sometimes implicit and sometimes much felt. Other readings also inspired by the phenomenological tradition, which have already been encountered in this book, can generate a description of the volume in a "beyond" and an "outside", therefore nearly inevitably entailing a shift of focus away from the entity itself. For example, referring to needs, thoughts or passions, Sartre writes that "they are always outside of themselves toward…" [SAR 63, p. 151]. The theory of the volume wants to express manifestly his consistency and stability: none of his voluments is outside him and wrenches the volumic reality away from itself. The volume is and remains a volume. Perceptions, the feeling or knowledge of oneself and the various modalities of consciousness are indeed voluments of the volume. They would not exist without a volume. I would like to add that they are merely elements of the volume just like any other, sometimes visible, sometimes invisible, mixed with these other elements, an action, a gesture, or a style and in various combinations. Could the theory of the volume not be in line with Lévi-Strauss? Some of its suspicious attributes, like the ego or freedom, have been removed. Feelings, including the most intense ones, lived experiences and the modes of consciousness have a clearly delimited place, and I insist on the need for meticulous and rigorous methods. Conceiving the human being as a volumic entity that has become the anthropological unity is a way of looking at him and having a methodological grip, without letting a theory of consciousness prevail or some lived experiences, thought to be inaccessible, become an obstacle. As I have mentioned above, the anthropology of the volume *only* needs every individual to speak in order to identify feelings and modes of consciousness, and it may require him to explicitate them in interviews carried out methodically, which are being considered and employed more and more today [PET 06]. A good way of seizing this part of the volume involves in this case microphenomenology or, better, microphenomenography, in connection with the cognitive sciences, and the implementation, as I have mentioned above, "of methods that make it possible to gather precise and rigorous data on a personal basis, namely expressing the point of view of the subject himself on his experience" [PET 15, p. 55]. Thus, the individual, helped by the interviewer and according to a work procedure that is well organized and clearly defined, may become aware of his "concrete memory". He can then explicitate implicit aspects, lived experiences and perceptions, some of which are directly relevant to the situation while others are secondary. Thus, I think that an anthropologist cannot bring himself to think that his research field is limited to the surface of the volumic entity.

1.2.3. Based on the structural explanation applied to the human being, even if only some main principles are kept – "the spirit over the letter" – and the experts in Lévi-Strauss' work are not satisfied with this treatment, there is a "methodological effect" or, rather, the possibility of understanding in more detail the human volume, such as I regard him. In any case, structural existantism aims to conceive, on the one hand, the distinct and compresent voluments of the volume, without resorting to an explanation on a different scale, which is reserved for other fields of study, and to conceive, on the other hand, the entity volume who requires an approach that is as exhaustive as possible and does not limit the number of these voluments, while also integrating them into this entirety.

1.3. The third point concerns volumuations. The goal is then to retrieve some way of volumuating, in most cases as gradations rather than contrasts or differences, and to understand the "internal cohesion" of the volume [LEV 96, p. 28]. Lévi-Strauss refers to "transformations", but this term, which has been already mentioned, may seem too strong if the aim is to describe volumuations or microvariations of the same volume instant after instant or at other intervals. Therefore, it is necessary to keep referring in a flexible way to the structural method, which highlights "divisions and contrasts" [LEV 62, p. 75], and avoid strictly applying its ways of dividing somewhat rigidly, reducing and classifying. On the contrary, I attempt to understand a volume's volumuations, which are always partial and sometimes hardly perceivable. Lévi-Strauss' analyses are centered on the transformations from one myth to another and from one kinship system to another. Beyond these transformations, Lévi-Strauss also points out that his goal is to understand internal cohesion. "Studying transformations, thanks to which we can find similar properties in systems that are superficially different" makes it possible to discover "an internal cohesion", which is "inaccessible when only an isolated system is observed" [LEV 96, p. 28]. When human volumes are compared, differences and similarities can appear, for example regarding logics or modalities that govern the variation but also the stability of the voluments and their compresences. This kind of analysis can then shed light on the modes of "internal cohesion", the ultimate horizon of the anthropology of the volumes. Of course, as I have repeated at length, focusing on the successive volumuations of the same volume is also a priority. In any case, it is important that comparing different "forms" does not entail a loss of details and an overhasty consideration of "the interrelation between entities" or "discontinuities" [LEV 63, p. 328], which would seem relevant, as Lévi-Strauss suggests. He also mentions D'Arcy Thompson, whom he presents as "a great naturalist" [LEV 63, p. 328] in order to reinforce his comparative reading: "In a very large part of morphology, our essential task lies in the comparison of related forms rather than in the precise definition of each" [LEV 63, p. 328]. These "related forms" may be those of a volume according to the moments and situations following one another. However, I would find it inconceivable not to describe with precision a "figure" and to situate it immediately in relevant contrasts. As can be seen, the risk of descriptive imprecision and loss of the volume is constant. I would say that the figure is the entire volume with his surface and internal voluments. He indeed remains the goal of the analysis, based on his components and their variations instant after instant, while attention is paid every time to what is left unchanged.

1.4. Lévi-Strauss states that in an analysis "some transformations are thrust into the background or become lost in the distance. They become confused and blurred or are glimpsed only intermittently" [LEV 69, p. 118]. Once again, the observer of human volumes should be cautious and pay heed to details, knowing that ongoing variations are combined with continuities. This is a renewed warning about not letting a single line of thinking take over and guide research. I also think that the types of transformations detected by Lévi-Strauss between myths or between kinship systems, rigid or not sufficiently precise (for example, permutation, substitution, replacement, inversion, conjunction, disjunction, but also symmetry, homology and a few more) do not truly allow an analysis of the microvariations of the human volume, which implies integrating the origin of the volumuation, its intensity and the voluments of the volume concerned. From this standpoint, it is useful to revisit some points discussed before in relation to volumuation. Let us recall that the issue involves conceiving first modalities related to how the volume volumuates and structures himself instead of external factors of change. It is possible to identify first a general dynamic in the volume in two ways. On the one hand, as has been seen before, an action is carried out and arises from the volume – from a specific volume – but it is not separate from him. This action is thus compresent with other voluments, like thoughts, feelings, social habits, a style, or some know-hows. These voluments pervade the origin and unfolding of the action, which may entail the expression of other voluments, for example, an emotion, or some affects, which in turn may involve other actions and a gradual change in mental scripts and thoughts, which remain associated with a specific stylistic tendency of the volume, and so on. On the other hand, voluments of other volumes, an action, a word or an emotion are perceived and then absorbed, and in some sort buried in the volume. They may in other cases have a direct effect and involve new actions, words or emotions, which are also pervaded by a style and know-hows. They can also affect social habits, perhaps nuance stylistic traits, modify know-hows, generate a new role or lead to adjustments of a former role, whose concretizations are pervaded by other stylistic expressions of the volume. All this may have some reverberations in a perhaps distant future, but these reverberations will probably not find expression outside the volume's character. In all these configurations, the figures of lessereity should also be identified. It is lessereity that lessens, diminishes, reduces and causes something to be forgotten, as has been shown. Then, from the overview of this general dynamic, I can define a terminology that helps me identify first the different modalities of volumuation that take shape, in each situation and at each moment, from external elements or events or through the movement of voluments based on the volume himself. Second, there are also the modalities that ensure the continuity of the volume, with the stability of voluments and their contents, which are sometimes well established and pervading, or which change only partially and not all at the same time, and third, what is involved in the lessening structuration of the volume. It would be from such types of observations that it would be possible to discover regularities in the volumuation and continuity logics as well as in the combinations between voluments[4]. In any case, these three logics are necessary to conceive the way in which the volume is structured. None of these three dimensions can be envisaged without the other two. Here is the terminology suggested.

For volumuation:

– *impact* refers to the immediate effect of an action, word and emotion on a specific volument, for example a gesture, word, mood or posture;

– *infiltration* defines a gradual effect on the volume and especially on a specific volument. The effects may linger or even be reversible. Infiltration, with the progressive nuances it involves, may also concern stylistic traits;

– *addition* indicates the presence of a new volument, which can be clearly identified in the volume, for example a role or a type of knowledge;

– *reverberation* is like the echo of an event in acts or thoughts, and its effect is less strong than that entailed by an impact or infiltration;

---

4 On the basis of and in addition to several detailed observations, I think that some mathematical formulations about the human volume and his volumuations are possible and even desirable, engaging in a dialog with Lévi-Strauss' algebraic intuitions about myths.

– *adjustment* defines the adaptation of one or more voluments to a situation, role, event, the voluments of other volumes, but also an intravolumic change. Adjustment can be temporary as well as lasting.

For continuity:

– *absorption* (or integration) indicates that the event or action that has emerged and been perceived, or their effect, is absorbed into the entirety of the volume, leaving few or no direct traces. Absorption is not necessarily immediate;

– *determination* refers to the force of the pervading voluments, for example a role, style, or social mark, on gestures, words, or other actions of the volume, leading to their emergence or marking modalities of accomplishing them. Determination in the same way defines the pervading force that appropriates what reaches the volume from outside, whether this is an event, an action or a word. Thus, some acts are in a way contained, retained and appropriated in the volume by a specific role, habit or stylistic trait;

– a typically social (associated with a family habit, for example, a gestural modality) or cultural trait and a stylistic characteristic (an expression of a mode of being present) may themselves pervade each other;

– as is well known, volumuations do not define effects on the entire volume but on some of his voluments. Since the dynamic governing these variations is partial and gradual, there are leftovers, and not only those that attenuate or leave an effect or a trace incomplete, but also voluments that are not concerned and do not change while others become involved in the movement of the volumuation.

For lessereity, it is necessary to mention the omnipresent figures that have been specified above and through which volumuations occur. For example:

– wandering thoughts, which create *presences–absences*, and incompletions are ways of attenuating, modulating, diminishing and not facing directly what should be done or what happens;

– *suspension* indicates that actions or emotions have not been "followed up" in the succession of instants;

– *hypolucidity* is possible through the non-mobilization of knowledge, rationality or consciousness;

– *oblivion* indicates that what has happened – thoughts, actions and emotions – has been at least buried;

– the mixture of habits and dispositions together with important actions or emotions may lead to decreases in intensity;

– the compresence of voluments entails another lessening effect that involves social or cultural traces and the style itself, among themselves or with other voluments, making these traces and the style less directly monolithic, as they do not express themselves totally every time and according to some of their specific traits.

1.5. Thus, it is possible to establish how the volume is structured. There is a triangular logic between three combined forces: those that create a volumuation (impact–addition–infiltration–reverberation–adjustment), those that mark, based on the volumuation, the continuity of the volume (determination–permeation–absorption–integration), and those that, concomitantly with the other two, lessen the intensity and make the succession of actions possible (these are the figures of lessereity). In fact, a volume cannot be imagined without these three interdependent and simultaneously unfolding forces, naturally in different proportions at specific times, in specific situations. It is an actual observational challenge to follow them as they become interconnected, moment after moment, and characterize the existence of the volume. As has been shown by the theoretical presentation of the volume (Chapter 1), the figures of lessereity are so permanently and generally important that I would say it is lessereity itself that regulates the other two forces. In the face of what is caused by the others in particular, the unity of the volume needs some specific figures of lessereity that make it possible to attenuate, forget, disintensify and appropriate, as has been seen. Without this element, the absorption, determination and stylistic appropriation enabled by the continuing force of the volume would not manage to regulate the variations, and continuity and change would be tensely contrasted. Lessereity, which affects itself the style and social dimension of the volume, ensures that the variation and continuity dynamics have some "plasticity", playing a part in the routinization through which the volume keeps up with the pace of the instants. It is meta-regulating and inherent in the volume, as if it controlled his unitary development, in the face of what happens and the various volumuations. I would say that lessereity is the "regulatory principle" of what Lévi-Strauss calls an actual "armature" in the volume [LEV 66, p. 359], which attenuates, discards and makes it possible to integrate or absorb what happens, regulate contradictions, with different degrees of traces, and simultaneously do and produce. Such is the volume with his actions and relations. They cannot be dissociated from the unity of the volume, and they are heavily dependent on and pervaded by his various characteristic voluments (like the role in the situation, social marks, or style); actions, whether the volume's own or those of other volumes, may affect him, but these impacts are only partial and reappropriated; through the various appropriation and distance effects concerning the actions and emotions within in the same unity; through its withdrawal into itself, the volumic entity imposes in any case its consistency to its voluments and the actions and relations that take shape.

1.6. These three regulating forces ensure the cohesion of the volume, which is concrete and perceivable, expressing itself just as the volume acts, speaks and thinks. This cohesion reveals that the human volume is not a mere collection of elements, as he is held together by a specific principle inherent in the existence of a volume. This sentence written by Montaigne refers to this point:

> Such as make it their business to oversee human actions, do not find themselves in anything so much perplexed as to reconcile them and bring them into the world's eye with the same lustre and reputation; for they commonly so strangely contradict one another that it seems impossible they should proceed from one and the same person. [MON 09, p. 409]

And slightly further on:

> We are all lumps, and of so various and shapeless a contexture, that every piece plays in every moment its own game, and there is as much difference betwixt us and ourselves as betwixt us and others. [MON 09, p. 417]

However, these "lumps" are not, as Montaigne indicates, part of a shapeless collection, ceaselessly generating differences. We have seen that the opposite is true: a volume determined by himself and regulated by lessereity, a style and habits that express themselves in actions, gestures or words, appropriates in his consistency "odds and ends" [LEV 62, p. 22] of events. Numerous voluments, with variable durations and modalities, are linked to him. At each moment, not all pieces are necessarily involved, but it is impossible for only a single lump to be active, as it will be at least pervaded by a style, various habits and states of mind. I would also say that contradictions are not random and do not conceal this style. As a kinship system and a myth are held together by a structure or an armature, as has been shown, the human volume is undoubtedly an entirety held together.

2. When he is challenged about the specificity of anthropology, Lévi-Strauss muddles up his explanation – for example in [LEV 58, p. 37 and ff.] – perceiving few differences between social anthropology and sociology, placing anthropology in a "nebula" [LEV 63, p. 347] or grouping it "with one or more of the following branches of study" [LEV 63, p. 359], admitting that "anthropology is not distinguished from other humanistic and social sciences by any subject of study peculiar to it alone" [LEV 63, p. 347], and considering it part of the natural sciences, the social sciences and the humanities. We return over and over again to the goal of anthropology, its project, but also its "object". Here, I have thus attempted to show that referring, in moderate or critical terms, to the idea of structure may help an anthropologist become an anthropologist who focuses on the human volume and his components and able to make comparisons in order to get as close as possible to the theoretical goal of anthropology. However, this structural existantism implies indeed an anthropological reversal. By placing the emphasis on the existing volume – who is there before most of the voluments that constitute him with their compresences – this reading makes it possible to provide tools and points of reference and give methodological and theoretical force to existantial anthropology, which differs then from philosophical existentialism.

3. I believe that setting this anthropological goal means looking for an "absolute": the human being for his own sake as he is a human being who is entire, not fragmented or reduced to some voluments, and not relegated to contextual backgrounds. "Absolute comes from *absolvere*, in its two clearly separate meanings: on the one hand, unbinding, undoing, releasing and liberating, and, on the other hand, completing and perfecting. *Absolutus* has always had the latter meaning" [LAL 09, p. 7]. This is not quite accurate since, according to Latin grammar, the ablative absolute refers to a clause that is detached from the sentence. It is a participial form syntactically detached from the sentence, which defines, often succinctly, a circumstance related to the main idea and takes the ablative, one of the cases of the Latin declensions. In mathematics, for example, the absolute value of numbers

does not depend on the sign (plus or minus). These two meanings are interesting. Absolute anthropology as existantism brings out the human being and claims, therefore, to have a radical goal, that is, to consider the human being as an entire and continuous volume. It is certainly not perfect and complete, nor will it ever be so. It asymptotically moves towards the volume who is before its eye. In so doing, this type of anthropology considers the human *nearly* independently of his relations and representations, especially those associated with the difference between the West and the others. These elements have guided the history of anthropology and most of its interpretive approaches, including today the critique of this opposition and the way of rehabilitating these "others". What constituted the first anthropological principle – cultural diversity – remains in fact central for the field of study, even if people say that anthropology is experiencing a crisis, that it is interested in the globalization of societies and that anthropologists are adopting ethnographic approaches in every possible situation in the world. These are not the choices I have made. Associating the future of anthropology with an "absolute", the human being whom the observer must radically face constitutes a clearly different approach and a whole other question. As I have pointed out, when compared with the other entities studied in the social sciences (institutions, collective systems, cultures, gods, situations, actions or experiences), the human volume is a less non-absolute being, as it were, on whom all these elements depend. It is nearly comical to imagine an action without a complete volume who carries it out, or a divine or institutional presence without human beings. More than his productions, which have their own field of study, the human being "deserves" his own too. This field of study would regard the human being as a "nominative absolute", which is not cut from the rest of the sentence but extracted from it, while also remaining retained to it by a thin thread that does not suck him up into the background. Anthropologists may well claim the argument of "the others" and "alterity". However, a human being appropriates and lessens the others in that he is a volumic entity. All this results in an anthropological imperative: not losing the scale of the human being instant after instant. It can be accepted that other fields of study lose this dimension and are not interested in it. I cannot bring myself to accept that anthropology forgets the scale of the human being and the continuous instants. I would like to point out once more that this is the basic anthropologicality of anthropology. I repeat this point, which we encountered in Lévi-Strauss' thinking. Singularity becomes meaningful only in relation to an instant, at most an existence, and no longer on the scale of the planet and the universe. Anthropology, focused on human beings, will not elude this "nothingness". In any case, either one claims that the word "anthropology" takes on a meaning as a field of study or one claims that it does not. However, if one wants to practice anthropology, one should do so in radical terms and not by bypassing the human being himself. Either there is anthropology or there is no anthropology.

Conclusion

Art as a Paradigm for Anthropology

1. In Rilke's words, "I am learning how to see. I'm starting. It's still not going well. But I want to make the most of my time" [RIL 16, p. 4]. Conceiving human beings and learning to look at them without sucking them up into other things is not easy, given how accustomed we are to looking at them and immediately losing them in search of other things. I read these words by Rilke as an encouragement to truly look at human beings without circumventing them. In this book, I have already mentioned Rilke as well as Hopkins, Manet and Rodin. Art and the works and writings of artists may in fact invite us to look at the human being and to reflect on such an approach. I will merely outline this contribution of art by way of conclusion. Today, art and anthropology are dialoguing in every sense, far from being centered on the human being, as if their harmony depended on putting him into brackets. On the contrary, I would like to insist on the artistic gaze as something that precedes the act of looking at human beings. In this sense, art, or more precisely the artistic way of looking, constitutes a didactic tool for conceiving anthropology as a science that radically looks at the human being[1]. These two modes of knowledge, art and anthropology, should not be hybridized. It is indeed in the distance of one from the other that art may become a paradigm, a model and an example for the anthropologist. By "paradigm", I refer to nothing more than a framework of ideas and practices. Art is a methodological, epistemological and thematic resource, an invitation for the anthropologist to be surprised by his habitual way of looking and to discover lines of thinking and research avenues. This does not apply to the entirety of art and to every artist and artwork. Here, I will only make some

---

1 Part of these reflections result directly from my conversations with Catherine Beaugrand.

references based on which I will improperly – if I may say so – talk about art and artists in general. Art and some artists could, by the way equally, be mentioned in order to learn not to look at the human being. However, what I find interesting is the artist's capacity to pause before things, in this case the human being, and look at this being while also extracting him from his context. Let us remember in this sense the remarks that Manet made before painting his "Fifer". I recall then that art is a way of working, an epistemological investigation, a quest for singularity and a capacity to perceive. I hope that the reader will notice the force of the shift in looking that art may bring about for the anthropologist. I will highlight a few points, made in particular by Rodin, Giacometti, Rilke and Bergson (in relation to art).

2. Artists look time and again, striving to observe, and always return to their work. I see in this some radical and necessary naivety. Literature can be said to concern often invented people and beings, but a specific painting or sculpture refers directly to a precise reality and a "model" before the eyes of the artist. This aspect should not be neglected. Giacometti points out that Rodin, who had a technical and geometric knowledge of the human body and his busts, adopted a fairly "objectivist" methodology: "he took measurements" and "he did not sculpt a head as he saw it, in space". His goal, as he worried about the reference of his model, was to draw "a concrete parallel, the exact equivalent of this volume in space" [GIA 90, p. 287]. Naturally, Rodin's work should not be reduced to this dimension. Concerning "the life" that inspired Rodin's work, Rilke wrote that the sculptor:

> Seized upon life as he saw it all around him. He observed it, cleaved to it, and laid hold of its most seemingly minor manifestations. He watched for it at moments of transition and hesitation, he overtook it in flight, and everywhere he found it equally great, equally powerful and enthralling. No part of the body was insignificant or trivial, for even the smallest of them was alive. [RIL 12, p. 22]

In his conversation with Gsell, Rodin pointed this out when he mentioned his models, who did not sit posing but walked around his atelier [ROD 84, p. 23 and ff.]. Gsell was astonished. Similarly, the anthropologist follows and looks at a volume of being. As Rodin is faced with the "continuous presence of undressed human beings who come and go", "his eyes follow his models. He savors silently the beauty of the life that plays in them" [ROD 84, p. 10]. He specifies that "the only principle in art is to copy what one sees [...]. It is only a question of seeing" [ROD 84, pp. 11–13]. The difference between a model whom the artist requires to be in a specific position and a model who can freely walk about the atelier is significant, all the more so for the anthropologist confronted with the movement of existence. However, in both cases we can see that some human beings are there, like a reality faced by the artist who is looking. Such is the force of what is implied by the idea of model. Let us say that the artist has dared to look at the human being. The following excerpt is another very relevant quote drawn from Giacometti:

> It is rather abnormal that instead of living one spends one's time trying to copy a head, immobilizing someone in a chair every afternoon, the same person for five years, trying to copy him without succeeding, and still going on. It's not an activity one could call exactly normal, do you think? [GIA 90, p. 278]

In any case, this is the opposite of what people in most cases do and also of the ethnographic viewpoint, which involves especially being with people, looking at groups, and scanning what happens with oscillating eyes.

2.1. In his correspondence and diaries, an artist may express his obsession with what he sees and his relentless way of facing the reality and materials with which he works, including methodological and epistemological details. He expresses a desire to get as close as possible to this or that reality, simultaneously questioning the difficulties of looking at and of the modalities to seize it. Among other works, Giacometti's *Écrits* in this sense have a radical force and become nearly a prerequisite to observe the human being. Giacometti is torn, tormented and ceaselessly in doubt: imitating, not imitating, copying, not copying, representing, not representing, depicting, not depicting, creating or not creating likeness – all this in the face of the movement of things, their distance, their depth and the screen possibly constituted by the artist's own vision. Such tensions and the questions they entail are in the service of an obsession: "Only reality interests me now and I know I could spend the rest of my life in copying a chair" [GIA 90, p. 98]. Giacometti goes on to say that "reality remains exactly as virgin and unknown as the first time anyone attempted to represent it" [GIA 90, p. 267]. A chair is one thing, but how can we not be "dazzled by people's faces" [GIA 90, p. 262]? Their face or the whole person? Giacometti believes that "what is essential is the head", but he also claims to be attempting to distance himself from particulars to "reach the universal", aiming for the architecture of the human face, yet also driven by the desire to seize this face to preserve it, as it is always threatened by the various identities that everyone wants to play. As he notes:

> The more a painting wants to represent reality, the more I am touched by those elements which at first sight do not seem to be the very signs of objects, but perhaps it is precisely these elements that end up recreating the vision of the object. [GIA 90, p. 69]

Is he not referring to the importance of secondary gestures, that is, those which ostensibly do not count? As he also points out:

> Heads and figures merely constitute constant internal and external movement, they ceaselessly change, they do not have an actual consistency […]. They are a moving mass, a changing form, and something never truly graspable. They are in some sort linked by an internal principle that looks at us in the eye and seems to be their reality. [GIA 90, p. 218]

We find again movement and constant variations. Faced with the impossibility of expressing movement, it is wise to "try every possibility anyway" [GIA 90, p. 188], as Giacometti writes. However, do volumes lack consistency? As he has pointed out, there is also a mass and "an internal principle", some stability, a style and some continuity [see DUF 10]. This is restated in the following excerpt:

> Even the most insignificant head, the least violent one, in the head of the fuzziest person, the flabbiest, in a deficient condition, if I start to try and draw that head, or paint it or sculpt it, the whole thing is transformed, becomes a tense form, and, it always seems to me, one with the most highly contained violence, as though the form itself of the person always exceeded what the person is. But he is also that: he is above all a sort of nucleus of violence. This is likely. It seems rather plausible to me that he is such for him to exist… due the very fact that he does exist, that he isn't ground up, crushed, it seems to me there has to be a force to keep him together! [GIA 90, p. 245]

2.2. The "internal principle that looks at us": this is why I do not think that Sartre's ideas are entirely correct. For him, Giacometti's sculptures express the human being as he is seen by others, "Man as they see him, as he is for other men, as he emerges among men" [SAR 82, p. 302], given that, as he insists, "he is the being whose essence involves existing for others". Undoubtedly, some of Giacometti's works and their own archaeology may confirm this point of view. I am thinking, in particular, about some drawings of people, drawn on the spot in a notebook, which show an interplay of lines that break and overlap, as if they indicated a visual "network of trajectories". Do these interwoven lines, which are always inside an outline, fail to provide consistency? It is here important to remember that, according to the approach developed in this book, the volume precedes lines. Giacometti adds about the passers-by he looks at and draws that "a man walking down the street is weightless" and that "his weight cannot be felt" (quoted in [GIA 18, p. 10]). However, this human does have a weight and consistency. For that matter, Charles Juliet acknowledges that Giacometti during his life only wanted to express "everything" about "Man and his condition", and that what seems "essential" to him is everyone's fragility and the energy required to go on and "remain standing" [JUL 07, p. 63]. This is what some of Giacometti's works show, a volume who looks, almost aware that he will not be seen, and attempts to face up, beyond the presence of the others. I think that Giacometti's "heads", as they emerge, are more radical than Sartre claims.

3. As something inherent in a focus on the volume, aiming for singularity seems equally important to me. I do not like to consider art and science as part of a dichotomy, assigning emotion to one and reason to the other. On the contrary, I have just pointed out the relentless work of artists and their well thought out relation to reality. Yet, a contrast highlighted by Bergson is interesting. Bergson emphasizes the detachment of the artist freed from the practical constraints of life and from an intellectual mode that selects and filters [BER 46, p. 62]. He pits him against the researcher who erases the "differences that are useless" and accentuates the "resemblances that are useful". This entails a loss of "the individuality of things or of beings" to the advantage of some traits, facilitating a "practical recognition" [BER 14, p. 152]. The philosopher criticizes the psychology that detaches and isolates "a psychological state in order to set it up as a more and less independent entity", disregarding thus "the person's special coloration" [BER 46, p. 200]. What I keep in mind from this is not the regret about how science lacks something reserved for art, but the fact that science must seize this

something, by remaining itself, that is, methodological and conceptual. Thus, the volumic approach takes this into account, and the anthropologist, reminded by art, finds his object par excellence. This is precisely the topic treated in this book. Commenting on Rodin's *The Man with the Broken Nose*, Rilke points out some details:

> We feel what moved Rodin to form this head, which is that of an aging, ugly man, whose broken nose only heightens the pained expression on his face. The fullness of life is gathered in these features, and there are absolutely no symmetrical planes on the face. Nothing is repeated, no spot remains empty, mute, or neutral. [RIL 12, p. 30]

There are several texts written by artists or commentaries of this kind. As part of my reflection, I only wish to express their instructive heuristic nature, which can question an observer of human beings. In his *A Treatise on Painting*, Leonardo da Vinci writes that "it is a very great fault in a painter to repeat the same motions in figures, and the same folds in draperies in the same composition, as also to make all the faces alike" [VIN 04, p. 48]. Was it not Michelangelo who claimed that it is silly to not realize that "the foot is more noble than the shoe" [RED 89, p. 95]? Odilon Redon mentions these words by Michelangelo that I like to recall:

> If I could today start over my instruction as a painter, I think that in order to grow and develop my abilities more I would make several copies of the human body: I would dissect him, analyze him, and model him. [RED 89, p. 17]

4. The "detached" artist seen by Bergson can also in some way broaden his perception:

> Why then, being detached from reality to a greater degree, does he manage to see in it more things? We should not understand why if the vision we ordinarily have of external objects and of ourselves were not a vision which we had been obliged to narrow and drain by our attachment to reality, our need for living and acting. As a matter of fact, it would be easy to show that the more we are preoccupied with living, the less we are inclined to contemplate, and that the necessities of action tend to limit the field of vision. [BER 46, p. 161]

Besides a potentially doubtful dichotomy, Bergson expresses the distinguishing feature of the artist, who reveals to the scientist something that he, as he is rooted in the tradition of his field, has not perceived or wanted to perceive. He wonders: "what is the goal of art, if not to reveal in nature itself and the mind, outside and within us, things that did not explicitly strike our sense and our consciousness?" Naturally, an anthropologist could discover these "other things" without this artistic digression. As Giacometti writes, "The one thing that may captivate us is to discover a new edge, a new space, the minor part of a new space, to perceive it in the dark, as the light hardly touches it" [GIA 90, p. 123]. In fact, art favors the invention and proposal of new themes that must be re-appropriated methodologically and conceptually. It inspires an anthropologist to broaden his horizons and especially, I wish to underline this, to place the emphasis on something that might have been neglected. This point may seem well known, but I would like to say that it has become a reality for me in my goal to carry out the anthropology of human beings. Thus, in any case, art remains art, and anthropology becomes anthropology.

Bibliography

[ABU 91] ABU-LUGHOD L., "Writing against culture", in Fox R.G. (ed.), *Recapturing Anthropology: Working in the Present*, School of American Research Press, Santa Fe, pp. 139–162, 1991.

[AGA 16] AGAMBEN G., *The Use of Bodies*, Stanford University Press, Stanford, 2016 [2014].

[DAL 89] D'ALEMBERT *et al.*, *Encyclopédie méthodique, Mathématiques*, Panckoucke, Paris, 1789.

[ARA 08] ARASSE D., *L'Homme en perspective*, Hazan, Paris, 2008.

[ARI 04] ARISTOTLE, *The Metaphysics,* Penguin Books, London, 2004.

[AUB 09] AUBENQUE P., *Le Problème de l'être chez Aristote*, PUF, Paris, 2009.

[AUG 09] AUGE M., *Non-Places. Introduction to an Anthropology of Supermodernity*, Verso Books, London, 2009 [1992].

[AZO 95] AZOUVI F., *Maine de Biran, La science de l'homme*, Vrin, Paris, 1995.

[BAU 15] BAUER M. *et al.*, "Le dessin à dessein", *Fonds régional d'art contemporain-Auvergne*, Clermont-Ferrand, France, 2015.

[BEA 17] BEAUGRAND C., "Continuité du volume d'être, vue de l'art", in PIETTE A., *Le Volume humain*, Le Bord de l'eau, Lormont, pp. 5–11, 2017.

[BEN 60] BENEDICT R., *Patterns of Culture*, Routledge, London, 1960.

[BER 14] BERGSON H., *Laugther. An Essay of the Meaning of the Comic*, The Macmillan Company, New York, 1914.

[BER 46] BERGSON H., *The Creative Mind*, The Philosophical Library, New York, 1946.

[BIE 05] BIEHL J., *Vita: Life in a Zone of Social Abandonment*, University of California Press, Berkeley, 2005.

[BIM 01] BIMBENET E., "'La chasse sans prise': Merleau-Ponty et le projet d'une science de l'homme sans l'homme", *Les Études philosophiques*, vol. 2, no. 57, pp. 239–259, 2001.

[BIM 17] BIMBENET E., *Le Complexe des trois singes, Essai sur l'animalité humaine*, Le Seuil, Paris, 2017.

[BLA 93] BLANCHOT M., *The Infinite Conversation*, University of Minnesota Press, Minneapolis, 1993 [1969].

[BLO 12] BLOCH M., *Anthropology and the Cognitive Challenge*, Cambridge University Press, Cambridge, 2012.

[BLU 00] BLUMENBERG H., *The Laughter of the Thracian Woman: A Protohistory of Theory*, Continuum Publishing Corporation, New York, 2000 [1987].

[BLU 11] BLUMENBERG H., *Description de l'homme*, Cerf, Paris, 2011.

[BOC 17] BOCQUET-APPEL J.-P., FORMOSO B., STEPANOFF C., "Pour une anthropologie générale. Crise et renouveau du partenariat scientifique et institutionnel de l'anthropologie biologique, l'anthropologie sociale et la préhistoire", *L'Homme*, no. 223–224, pp. 221–246, 2017.

[BOL 06] BOLTANSKI L., THÉVENOT L., *On Justification: Economies of worth*, Princeton University Press, Princeton, 2006 [1991].

[BOU 90] BOURDIEU P., *The Logic of Practice*, Polity Press, Cambridge, 1990 [1980].

[BOU 77] BOURDIEU P., *Outline of a Theory of Practice*, Cambridge University Press, Cambridge, 1977 [1972].

[CAH 10] CAHOUR B., LICOPPE C. (eds), "Confrontations aux traces de son activité", *Revue d'anthropologie des connaissances*, vol. 4, no. 2, pp. 243–253, 2010.

[CAN 15] CANDEA M. (ed.), *Detachment: Essays on the Limits of the Relational Thinking*, Manchester University Press, Manchester, 2015.

[CAM 05] CAMPBELL N.A., REECE J.B., *Biology*, Pearson, San Francisco, 2005.

[CAN 08] CANGUILHEM G., *Knowledge of Live*, Fordham University Press, New York, 2008 [1965].

[CAR 13] CARROY J., RICHARD N., VATIN F. (eds), *L'Homme des sciences de l'homme, Une approche transdisciplinaire*, Presses universitaires de Paris Ouest, Nanterre, 2013.

[CAS 16] CASSOU-NOGUES P., *Métaphysique d'un bord de mer*, Cerf, Paris, 2016.

[CRA 80] CRAPANZANO V., *Tuhami: Portait of a Maroccan*, The University of Chicago Press, Chicago, 1980.

[CSO 94] CSORDAS T. (ed.), *Embodiment and Experience: The Existential Ground of Culture and Self*, Cambridge University Press, Cambridge, 1994.

[DAM 00] DAMISCH H., *The Origin of Perspective*, The MIT Press, Cambridge, 2000.

[DEC 01] DECLERCK P., *Les Naufragés*, Plon, Paris, 2001.

[DEL 05] DELEUZE G., GUATTARI F., *A Thousand Plateaus*, University of Minnesota Press, Minneapolis, 2005 [1980].

[DEN 15] DENIZEAU L., "Considering human existence: an existential reading of Michael Jackson and Albert Piette", in JACKSON M.D., PIETTE A. (eds), *What is Existential Anthropology?*, Berghahn, New York, pp. 214–236, 2015.

[DEP 14] DEPRAZ N., *Attention et Vigilance*, PUF, Paris, 2014.

[DES 13] DESCOLA P., *Beyond Nature and Culture*, University of Chicago Press, Chicago, 2013 [2006].

[DIA 94] DIAS N., "Photographier et mesurer : les portraits anthropologiques", *Romantisme*, vol. 84, pp. 37–49, 1994.

[DUF 10] DUFAY S., "Retrouver la face : étude du visage dans les dessins d'Antonin Artaud et d'Alberto Giacometti", in FLAHUTEZ F. (ed.), *Visage et Portrait, visage ou portrait*, Presses Universitaires de Paris Ouest, Nanterre, 2010.

[DUR 08] DURKHEIM E., *The Elementary Forms of Religious Life*, Dover Publications, New York, 2008 [1912].

[EME 83] EMERSON R.W., *First and Second Series*, Houghton Mifflin Company, Boston, 1883.

[FOU 05] FOUCAULT M., *The Order of Things*, Routledge, London, 2005 [1966].

[FUC 16] FUCHS T., "Self across time: the diachronic unity of bodily existence", *Phenomenology and the Cognitive Sciences*, no. 15, pp. 291–315, 2016.

[GAR 67] GARFINKEL H., *Studies in Ethnomethodology*, Prentice-Hall, Englewoods Cliffs, 1967.

[GIA 90] GIACOMETTI A., *Écrits*, Hermann, Paris, 1990.

[GIA 18] GIACOMETTI A., *À travers Paris*, Fondation Giacometti, Paris, 2018.

[GOD 03] GODEFROY F., *Lexique de l'ancien français*, Honoré Champion, Paris, 2003.

[GOE 52] GOETHE J.W. von, *Goethe's Botanical Writings*, University of Hawaii Press, Honolulu, 1952.

[GOE 98] GOETHE J.W. von, *Maxims and Reflections*, Penguin Classics, London, 1998.

[GOF 67] GOFFMAN E., *Interaction Ritual: Essays in Face-to-Face Behavior*, Aldine Pub. Co, Chicago, 1967.

[GRO 80] GROETHUYSEN B., *Anthropologie philosophique*, Gallimard, Paris, 1980.

[GUI 17] GUIMBAIL D., "Présentation de l'édition française", in PLESSNER H. (ed.), *Les Degrés de l'organique et l'Homme*, Gallimard, Paris, pp. 8–31, 2017.

[HAL 02] HALLÉ F., *In Praise of Plants*, Timber Press, Portland, 2002 [1999].

[HAM 07] HAMOU P., *La Vision perspective*, Payot, Paris, 2007.

[HEI 10] HEIDEGGER M., *Being and Time*, State University of New York Press, Albany, 2010 [1927].

[HEI 62] HEIDEGGER, M., *Kant and the Problems of Metaphysics*, Indiana University Press, Bloomington, 1962 [1929].

[HEI 66] HEIDEGGER, M., *Discourse on Thinking*, Harper and Row, New York, 1966.

[HEI 15a] HEISS J.P., *Musa: An Essay (or Experiment) in the Anthropology of the Individual*, Duncker & Humblot, Berlin, 2015.

[HEI 15b] HEISS J.P., PIETTE A., "Individuals in anthropology", *Zeitschrift für Ethnologie*, vol. 140, no. 1, pp. 5–17, 2015.

[HOP 59] HOPKINS G.M., *The Journals and Papers of Gerard Manley Hopkins*, Oxford University Press, Oxford, 1959.

[HUS 80] HUSSERL E., *Ideas Pertaining to a Pure Phenomenology and to a Phenomenological Philosophy, Second Book*, Kluwer Academic Publishers, Dordrecht, 1980.

[HUS 01] HUSSERL E., *Analyses Concerning Passive and Active Synthesis: Lectures on Transcendental Logic*, Springer, Dordrecht, 2001 [1918–1926].

[HUS 09] HUSSERL E., *Phénoménologie de l'attention*, Vrin, Paris, 2009.

[ING 90] INGOLD T., "An anthropologist at biology", *Man*, vol. 25, no. 2, pp. 208–229, 1990.

[ING 00] INGOLD T., *The Perception of the Environment*, Routledge, London, 2000.

[ING 11] INGOLD T., *Being Alive: Essays on Movement, Knowledge and Description*, Routledge, London, 2011.

[ING 13a] INGOLD T., *Making: Anthropology, Archaeology, Art and Architecture*, Routledge, London, 2013.

[ING 13b] INGOLD T., *Marcher avec les dragons*, Zones sensibles, Brussels, 2013.

[ING 13c] INGOLD T., PALSSON G. (eds), *Biosocial Becomings: Integrating Social and Biological Anthropology*, Cambridge University Press, Cambridge, 2013.

[ING 14] INGOLD T., "That's enough about ethnography", *Hau: Journal of Ethnographic Theory*, vol. 4, no. 1, pp. 383–395, 2014.

[ING 16] INGOLD T., "On human correspondance", *Journal of the Royal Anthropological Institute*, vol. 23, pp. 9–27, 2016.

[ING 18] INGOLD T., *Anthropology: Why it Matters*, Polity Press, Cambridge, 2018.

[JAC 15] JACKSON M.D., PIETTE A. (eds), *What is Existential Anthropology?*, Berghahn, New York, 2015.

[JAC 16] JACKSON M.D., *As Wide as the World is Wise*, Columbia University Press, New York, 2016.

[JEN 12] JENSEN C., "Anthropology as a following science", *NatureCulture*, vol. 1, no. 1, pp. 1–24, 2012.

[JUL 07] JULIET C., *Giacometti*, P.O.L., Paris, 2007.

[KEA 16] KEANE W., *Ethical Life*, Princeton University Press, Princeton, 2016.

[KNE 19] KNEUBÜHLER M., PIETTE A., "Following and analyzing a human being: on the continuity and singularity of an individual", in COOREN F., MALBOIS F. (eds), *How to Follow and Analyze...*, Routledge, London, pp. 13–43, 2019.

[LAL 09] LALANDE A., *Vocabulaire technique et critique de la philosophie*, PUF, Paris, 2009.

[LAT 87] LATOUR B., *Science in Action. How to Follow Scientists and Engineers through Society,* Harvard University Press, Harvard, 1987.

[LAT 94] LATOUR B., "Les objets ont-ils une histoire? Rencontre de Pasteur et de Whitehead dans un bain d'acide lactique", in BREUVART J.-M., COBB JR J.B., GRIFFIN D.R., Stengers I. (eds), *L'Effet Whitehead*, Vrin, Paris, pp. 196–217, 1994.

[LEJ 89] LEJEUNE P., *On Autobiography*, University of Minnesota Press, Minneapolis, 1989.

[LEV 61] LÉVI-STRAUSS C., *Tristes Tropiques*, Criterion Books, New York, 1961 [1955].

[LEV 62] LÉVI-STRAUSS C., *The Savage Mind*, Weidenfeld and Nicolson, London, 1962.

[LEV 63] LÉVI-STRAUSS C., *Structural Anthropology*, Basic Books, New York, 1963 [1958].

[LEV 69] LÉVI-STRAUSS C., *The Raw and the Cooked*, The University of Chicago Press, Chicago, 1969 [1964].

[LEV 77] LÉVI-STRAUSS C., *Structural Anthropology*, Vol. 2, Allen Lane, London, 1977 [1973].

[LEV 87] LÉVI-STRAUSS C., *Introduction to the Work of Marcel Mauss*, Routledge, London, 1987 [1950].

[LEV 90] LÉVI-STRAUSS C., *The Naked Man*, The University of Chicago Press, Chicago, 1990 [1971].

[LEV 91] LÉVI-STRAUSS C., *Totemism*, Merlin Press, London, 1991 [1962].

[LEV 96] LÉVI-STRAUSS C., *Anthropologie Structurale Deux*, Plon, Paris, 1996.

[LEV 78] LEVINAS E., *Existence and Existents*, Martinus Nijhoff, The Hague, 1978.

[LEW 15] LEWIS D., PARFIT D., SWINBURNE R., *Identité et Survie*, Ithaque, Paris, 2015.

[LIN 36] LINTON R., *The Science of Man*, Appleton-Century Crofts, New York, 1936.

[LIN 45] LINTON R., *The Cultural Background of the Personality*, Appleton-Century Crofts, New York, 1945.

[LUC 15] LUCHT H., "The station hustle: Ghanaian migration brokerage in a disjointed world", in JACKSON M.D., PIETTE A. (eds), *What is Existential Anthropology?*, Berghahn, New York, pp. 104–124, 2015.

[MAL 22] MALINOWSKI B., *Argonauts of the Western Pacific*, London, Routledge, 1922.

[MAU 50] MAUSS M., *Sociologie et Anthropologie*, PUF, Paris, 1950.

[MAU 04] MAUSS M., "Fait social et formation du caractère", *Sociologie et sociétés*, vol. 36, no. 2, pp. 135–140, 2004.

[MER 64] MERLEAU-PONTY M., *Signs*, Northwestern University Press, Evanston, 1964 [1960].

[MER 68] MERLEAU-PONTY M., *The Visible and the Invisible*, Northwestern University Press, Evanston, 1968 [1964].

[MER 73] MERLEAU-PONTY M., *The Prose of the World*, Northwestern University Press, Evanston, 1973 [1969].

[MER 05] MERLEAU-PONTY M., *Phenomenology of Perception*, Routledge, London, 2005 [1945].

[MIC 97] MICHAUX H., *Darkness Moves: An Henri Michaux Anthology, 1927–1984*, University of California Press, Berkeley, 1997.

[MIC 01] MICHAUX H., *Emergences/Resurgences*, Skiro, Milano, 2001.

[MON 03] MONTAIGNE M. de, *The Complete Essays*, Penguin Books, London, 2003.

[MUR 53] MURDOCH I., *Sartre: Romanic Rationalist*, Yale University Press, New Haven, 1953.

[NAB 58] NABOKOV V., "Scenes from the life of a double monster. A short story", *The Reporter*, vol. 1958, pp. 34–36, 1958.

[OXF 10] OXFORD UNIVERSITY PRESS, *Oxford Dictionary of English*, Oxford University Press, Oxford, 2010.

[OXF 12] OXFORD UNIVERSITY PRESS, *Oxford Latin Dictionary*, Oxford University Press, Oxford, 2012.

[PAL 13a] PALSSON G., "Ensembles of biosocial relations", in INGOLD T., PALSSON G. (eds), *Biosocial Becomings*, Cambridge University Press, Cambridge, pp. 22–41, 2013.

[PAL 13b] PALSSON G., "Retrospect", in INGOLD T., PALSSON G. (eds), *Biosocial Becomings*, Cambridge University Press, Cambridge, pp. 229–248, 2013.

[PAN 91] PANOFSKY E., *Perspective as Symbolic Form*, Zone books, New York, 1991.

[PER 08] PERREAU L., "La question de l'individu et de l'individuation chez Husserl", in TINLAND O. (ed.), *L'Individu*, Vrin, Paris, pp. 77–98, 2008.

[PET 06] PETITMENGIN C., "Describing one's subjective experience in the second person. An interview method for the science of consciousness", *Phenomenology and the Cognitive Sciences*, no. 5, pp. 229–269, 2006.

[PET 15] PETITMENGIN C., BITBOL M., OLLAGNIER-BELDAME M., "Vers une science de l'expérience vécue", *Intellectica*, vol. 64, pp. 53–76, 2015.

[PIE 92] PIETTE A., *Le Mode mineur de la réalité, Paradoxes et photographies en anthropologie*, Peeters, Leuven, 1992.

[PIE 96] PIETTE A., *Ethnographie de l'action, L'observation des détails*, Métailié, Paris, 1996.

[PIE 09] PIETTE A., *Anthropologie existentiale*, Pétra, Paris, 2009.

[PIE 10] PIETTE A., "The visual traces of an ethnographic investigation; or, how do people present themselves in a concrete situation?", *Visual Anthropology*, vol. 23, no. 3, pp. 186–199, 2010.

[PIE 13a] PIETTE A., *L'origine de la croyance*, Berg International, Paris, 2013.

[PIE 13b] PIETTE A., "Au cœur de l'activité, au plus près de la présence", *Réseaux. Communication-Technologie-Société*, vol. 182, pp. 57–88, 2013.

[PIE 14a] PIETTE A., *Contre le relationnisme*, Le Bord de l'eau, Lormont, 2015.

[PIE 14b] PIETTE A., *Avec Heidegger contre Heidegger, Introduction à une anthropologie de l'existence*, L'Âge d'homme, Lausanne, 2014.

[PIE 15] PIETTE A., *Existence in the Details: Theory and Methodology in Existential Anthropology*, Duncker & Humblot, Berlin, 2015.

[PIE 16] PIETTE A., *Separate Humans: Anthropology, Existence, Ontology*, Mimesis International, Milan, 2016.

[PIE 17a] PIETTE A., *Le Volume humain, Esquisse pour une science de l'homme*, Le Bord de l'eau, Lormont, 2017.

[PIE 17b] PIETTE A., "Theoretical principles of anthropology as a science of human beings", *Yearbook in Cosmopolitan Studies*, vol. 3, 2017.

[PIN 17a] DE PINA-CABRAL J., *World: An Anthropological Examination*, Hau Books Chicago, Chicago, 2017.

[PIN 17b] DE PINA-CABRAL J., "La transcendance de la compagnie. L'entre-aide parmi voisins et parents à Bahia (NE Brésil)", Working document, University of Kent, 2017.

[PLE 17] PLESSNER H., *Les Degrés organiques de l'homme, Introduction à une anthropologie philosophique*, Gallimard, Paris, 2017 [1928].

[PLE 70] PLESSNER H., *Laughing and Crying. A Study of the Limits of Human Behavior*, Northwestern University Press, Evanston, 1970 [1941].

[PRO 12] PROCHIANTZ A., *Qu'est-ce que le vivant?*, Le Seuil, Paris, 2012.

[RAD 52] RADCLIFFE- BROWN A.R., *Structure and Function in Primitive Society*, The Free Press, Glencoe, 1952.

[RAM 15] RAM K., HOUSTON C. (eds), *Phenomenology in Anthropology: a Sense of Perspective*, Indiana University Press, Bloomington, 2015.

[RAP 99] RAPPORT N., "The narrative as fieldwork technique", in AMIT V. (ed.), *Constructing the Field: Ethnographic Fieldwork in the Contemporary World,* Routledge, London, pp. 71–95, 1999.

[RAP 03] RAPPORT N., *I am Dynamite: An Alternative Anthropology of Power*, Routledge, London, 2003.

[RAP 15] RAPPORT N., "Anthropology through Levinas. Knowing the uniqueness of ego and the mystery of otherness", *Current Anthropology*, vol. 56, no. 2, pp. 256–276, 2015.

[RED 89] REDON O., *À soi-même*, José Corti, Paris, 1989.

[REE 18] REED A., BIALECKI J., "Introduction to special section 1: anthropology and the character", *Social Anthropology*, pp. 159–167, 2018.

[REM 03] REMY C., "Activité sociale et latéralisation. Pour une étude micro-ethnographique de la tension détermination/marge de manœuvre", *Recherches sociologiques*, vol. XXXIV, no. 3, pp. 95–113, 2003.

[RIL 62] RILKE R.M., *Letters to a Young Poet*, Norton & Company, New York: 1962 [1903–1908].

[RIL 09] RILKE R.M., *Notes of the Melody of Things*, 2009 [1955–1966], available at https://pen.org/notes-on-the-melody-of-things/.

[RIL 12] RILKE R.M., *Auguste Rodin*, Parkstone International, New York, 2012 [1903].

[RIL 16] RILKE R.M., *The Notebooks of Malte Laurids Brigge,* Oxford University Press, Oxford, 2016 [1910].

[ROD 84] RODIN A., *Art. Conversations with Paul Gsell,* University of California Press, Berkeley, 1984 [1911].

[ROM 10] ROMANO C., *Au cœur de la raison, la phénoménologie*, Gallimard, Paris, 2010.

[SAR 56] SARTRE J.-P., *Being and Nothingness*, Philosophical Library, New York, 1956 [1943].

[SAR 63] SARTRE J.-P., *Search for a Method*, Alfred A. Knopf, New York, 1963.

[SAR 87] SARTRE J.-P., *The Family Idiot*, Vol. 2, The Chicago University Press, Chicago, 1987 [1971–1972].

[SAU 98] SAUSSURE F. de, *Course in General Linguistics*, Open Court, Chicago, 1998.

[SIM 10] SIMMEL G., "How is society possible", *American Journal of Sociology*, vol. 16, no. 3, pp. 372–391, 1910.

[SOM 13] SOMMER C., "Métaphysique du vivant. Note sur la différence zoo-anthropologique de Plessner à Heidegger", *Philosophie*, vol. 1, no. 116, pp. 48–77, 2013.

[SUD 08] SUDAKA-BENAZERAF J., *Car le blanc seul n'est rien, Paul Klee illustrateur de Voltaire*, Ides et Calendes, Neuchâtel, 2008.

[TAR 02] TARDE G., *Psychologie économique*, vol. 1, Alcan, Paris, 1902.

[TAR 12] TARDE G., *Monadology and Sociology*, Re.press, Victoria, 2012.

[TAU 11] TAUSSIG M., *I Swear I Saw This: Drawing in Fieldwork Notebooks, Namely My Own*, University of Chicago Press, Chicago, 2011.

[TES 86] TESTART A. (ed.), "L'objet de l'anthropologie sociale", *Anthropologie: état des lieux*, Le Livre de Poche, Paris, pp. 147–150, 1986.

[THR 18] THROOP J., "Being Open to the World", *Hau*, vol. 8, no. 1/2, pp. 197–210, 2018.

[TON n.d.] TONDEUR K., "Le boom graphique en anthropologie. Histoire, contextes et chantiers du dessin anthropologique", n.d.

[TOR 02] TOREN C., "Anthropology as the whole science of what it is to be human science", in FOX R.G., KING B.J. (eds), *Anthropology beyond Culture*, Berg, Oxford, pp. 105–124, 2002.

[TOR 04] TOREN C., "Becoming a Christian in Fiji: an ethnographic study of ontogeny", *Journal of the Royal Anthropological Institute*, vol. 10, no. 1, pp. 222–240, 2004.

[TOR 12] TOREN C., "Anthropology and psychology", in FARDON R. (ed.), *The Sage Handbook of Social Anthropology,* vol. 1, Sage, Los Angeles, pp. 24–41, 2012.

[VAL 60] VALÉRY P., *Collected Works. Degas, Manet, Morisot (vol. 12)*, Princeton University Press, Princeton, 1960.

[VAL 77] VALÉRY P., "Man and the sea shell", in Valéry P. (ed.), *An Anthology,* Princeton University Press, Princeton, pp. 108–135, 1977.

[VAR 79] VARELA F., *Principles of Biological Autonomy,* Elsevier, New York, 1979.

[VAR 89] VARELA F., *Autonomie et Connaissance, Essai sur le vivant*, Le Seuil, Paris, 1989.

[VAR 99] VARELA F., *Ethical Know-How. Action, Wisdom and Cognition*, Stanford University Press, Stanford, 1999.

[VAR 04] VARELA F., *Quel savoir pour l'éthique ? Action, sagesse et cognition*, La Découverte, Paris, 2004.

[VER 99a] VERMERSCH P., "Introspection as practice", *Journal of Consciousness Studies*, vol. 6, nos. 2–3, pp. 17–42, 1999.

[VER 99b] VERMERSCH P., "Husserl et la méthode des exemples: application à l'étude d'un vécu émotionnel", *Expliciter*, no. 31, pp. 3–23, 1999.

[VER 18] VERMERSCH P., *The Explicitation Interview*, 2018 [1994], available at: https://www.researchgate.net/publication/324976173_The_explicitation_interview.

[VIN 04] VINCI L. DA, *A Treatise on Painting by Leonardo Da Vinci*, Kessinger Publishing, Whitefish, 2004 [1651].

[WAR 18] WARDLE H., "'Characters… Stamped upon the mind'. On the a priority of character in the Caribbean everyday", *Social Anthropology*, vol. 26, no. 3, pp. 314–329, 2018.

[WEB 16] WEBER A.-G., "La forme des nuages: science et poésie au tournant des XVIIIe et XIXe siècles", *Revue de littérature comparée*, vol. 3, no. 259, pp. 271–290, 2016.

[WEN 18] WENTZER T., MATTINGLY C., "Toward a new humanism. An approach from philosophical anthropology", *Hau*, vol. 8, no. 1/2, pp. 144–157, 2018.

[WIK 90] WIKAN U., *Managing Turbulent Hearts: A Balinese Formula for Living*, University of Chicago Press, Chicago, 1990.

[WIL 12] WILLEN S., SEEMAN D., "Introduction: experience and inquiétude", *Ethos*, vol. 40, no. 1, pp. 1–23, 2012.

[WIN 84] WINNICOTT D.W., *The Maturational Processes and the Facilitating Environment*, Karnac Books, London, 1984.

[WOO 02] WOOLF V., *Moments of being. Autobiographical Writings*, Pimlico, London, 2002.

[ZOU 94] ZOURABICHVILI F., *Deleuze, Une philosophie de l'événement*, PUF, Paris, 1994.

Index

Other titles from

in

Science, Society and New Technologies

2019

DESCHAMPS Jacqueline
Mediation. A Concept for Information and Communication Sciences
(Concepts to Conceive 21st Century Society Set – Volume 1)

DUPONT Olivier
Power
(Concepts to Conceive 21st Century Society Set – Volume 2)

GUAAYBESS Tourya
The Media in Arab Countries: From Development Theories to Cooperation
Policies

LARROCHE Valérie
The Dispositif
(Concepts to Conceive 21st Century Society Set – Volume 3)

LATERRASSE Jean
Transport and Town Planning: The City in Search of Sustainable
Development

2018

BARTHES Angela, CHAMPOLLION Pierre, ALPE Yves
Evolutions of the Complex Relationship Between Education and Territories
(Education Set - Volume 1)

BÉRANGER Jérôme
The Algorithmic Code of Ethics: Ethics at the Bedside of the Digital
Revolution
(Technological Prospects and Social Applications Set – Volume 2)

DUGUÉ Bernard
Time, Emergences and Communications
(Engineering, Energy and Architecture Set – Volume 4)

GEORGANTOPOULOU Christina G., GEORGANTOPOULOS George A.
Fluid Mechanics in Channel, Pipe and Aerodynamic Design Geometries 1
(Engineering, Energy and Architecture Set – Volume 2)

GEORGANTOPOULOU Christina G., GEORGANTOPOULOS George A.
Fluid Mechanics in Channel, Pipe and Aerodynamic Design Geometries 2
(Engineering, Energy and Architecture Set – Volume 3)

GUILLE-ESCURET Georges
Social Structures and Natural Systems: Is a Scientific Assemblage
Workable?
(Social Interdisciplinarity Set – Volume 2)

LARINI Michel, BARTHES Angela
Quantitative and Statistical Data in Education: From Data Collection to
Data Processing
(Education Set – Volume 2)

LELEU-MERVIEL Sylvie
Informational Tracking
(Traces Set – Volume 1)

SALGUES Bruno
Society 5.0: Industry of the Future, Technologies, Methods and Tools
(Technological Prospects and Social Applications Set – Volume 1)

TRESTINI Marc
Modeling of Next Generation Digital Learning Environments: Complex Systems Theory

2017

ANICHINI Giulia, CARRARO Flavia, GESLIN Philippe, GUILLE-ESCURET Georges
Technicity vs Scientificity – Complementarities and Rivalries
(Social Interdisciplinarity Set – Volume 2)

DUGUÉ Bernard
Information and the World Stage – From Philosophy to Science, the World of Forms and Communications
(Engineering, Energy and Architecture Set – Volume 1)

GESLIN Philippe
Inside Anthropotechnology – User and Culture Centered Experience
(Social Interdisciplinarity Set – Volume 1)

GORIA Stéphane
Methods and Tools for Creative Competitive Intelligence

KEMBELLEC Gérald, BROUDOUS EVELYNE
Reading and Writing Knowledge in Scientific Communities– Digital Humanities and Knowledge Construction

MAESSCHALCK Marc
Reflexive Governance for Research and Innovative Knowledge
(Responsible Research and Innovation Set - Volume 6)

PARK Sejin, GUILLE-ESCURET Georges
*Sociobiology vs Socioecology – Consequences of an Unraveling Debate
(Interdisciplinarity between Biological Sciences and Social Sciences Set -
Volume 1)*

PELLÉ Sophie
*Business, Innovation and Responsibility
(Responsible Research and Innovation Set - Volume 7)*

2016

BRONNER Gérald
Belief and Misbelief Asymmetry on the Internet

EL FALLAH SEGHROUCHNI Amal, ISHIKAWA Fuyuki, HÉRAULT Laurent,
TOKUDA Hideyuki
Enablers for Smart Cities

GIANNI Robert
*Responsibility and Freedom
(Responsible Research and Innovation Set - Volume 2)*

GRUNWALD Armin
*The Hermeneutic Side of Responsible Research and Innovation
(Responsible Research and Innovation Set - Volume 5)*

LAGRANA Fernando
*E-mail and Behavioral Changes – Uses and Misuses of Electronic
Communications*

LENOIR Virgil Cristian
*Ethical Efficiency – Responsibility and Contingency
(Responsible Research and Innovation Set - Volume 1)*

MAESSCHALCK Marc
*Reflexive Governance for Research and Innovative Knowledge
(Responsible Research and Innovation Set - Volume 6)*

PELLÉ Sophie, REBER Bernard
From Ethical Review to Responsible Research and Innovation
(Responsible Research and Innovation Set - Volume 3)

REBER Bernard
Precautionary Principle, Pluralism and Deliberation – Sciences and Ethics
(Responsible Research and Innovation Set - Volume 4)

VENTRE Daniel
Information Warfare – 2nd edition